Paper Flower Sculpture

JEANNE WESTCOTT

Paper Flower Sculpture

with line illustrations by the author
and colour photography by Steve Bicknell ABIPP

BLANDFORD PRESS
POOLE · NEW YORK · SYDNEY

First published in the UK 1986 by Blandford Press,
Link House, West Street, Poole, Dorset, BH15 1LL

Distributed in the United States by
Sterling Publishing Co., Inc.,
2 Park Avenue, New York, N.Y. 10016

Distributed in Australia by
Capricorn Link (Australia) Pty Ltd.,
PO Box 665, Lane Cove, NSW 2066

ISBN 0 7137 1673 8 Hardback
ISBN 0 7137 1674 6 Paperback

British Library Cataloguing in Publication Data

Westcott, Jeanne
  Paper flower sculpture.
  1. Paper flowers
  I. Title
  745.594'3   TT892

Typeset by Poole Typesetting (Wessex) Ltd.
Printed in Great Britain by R. J. Acford, Chichester

I dedicate this book to my husband Herrick
who has been a constant source of encouragement

Contents

Preface

A desire to share my good fortune has prompted me to write this book. Having always had a great admiration for nature's handiwork, the beautiful construction of flowers constantly gives me great pleasure. I have been blessed with a keen, observant eye and a gift for recreating in paper the flowers I see. The results of several years hard work and dedication are here and I know the book will give endless pleasure and satisfaction to anyone who enjoys a challenge!

Anyone wanting to make paper flowers has to have patience and a wish to succeed. Having said this, the instructions are very clear and concise. Age is no barrier as I have taught Paper Flower Sculpture for the past five years to adults (including men), in ages ranging from twenty to eighty-one!

The incredibly life-like flowers are often mistaken for real — each bloom is a work of art. Your friends will not believe they are made from *paper*! This is an inexpensive craft which will occupy many hours and, at the end, the reader should look at flowers with a new eye.

Acknowledgements

Thanks are due to Steve Bicknell for his colour photography of the finished flowers and to Chartwell Illustrators for their work on the annotations to my line illustrations.

Also I sincerely thank all those students who checked the accuracy of the flowers and assisted in the publication of this book.

1. Equipment and Special Techniques

BASIC TOOLS AND PAPERS

The following information will be useful before commencing to make any of the flowers in this book.

Scissors   These are very important, you need two pairs, one small pair with sharp points and, likewise, a larger pair.

Adhesive   A non-toxic latex-type with plastic spatula for application, is the type of adhesive which is recommended for best results. In Britain, Copydex is the product to use. The lid of a glass jar is useful to put the adhesive out ready for use.

Ruler (12 inch)   A non-see-through plastic ruler with a sharp straight edge is best. Wooden rulers are not so good.

Pliers   A small pair suitable for bending and cutting wire.

Thin cardboard   The back of a cereal packet will do. This is used for pattern templates only. Where other cardboard is mentioned it can be obtained from an art shop.

Lead pencil (B)

Tracing paper   Greaseproof paper will do here.

Stem wires   I use two thicknesses of green plastic-covered garden wire, obtained from a garden centre or shop. The two thicknesses are 2 mm and $1\frac{1}{4}$ mm, the former is used more often.

Rose wires   Very fine wire, similar to fuse wire, obtained from a florist. Usually sold in packets of 100 wires, each is about 7 in long (0.32 mm thickness). Florists' wires 7 in long of 0.9 mm thickness are used for rhododendron leaves only.

Pastel crayons   I use conté, but there are other varieties which are equally satisfactory. (A small piece of cotton wool soaked in white spirit will remove grease from the point of the crayon, thus giving improved colouring results.) Oil-based pastel crayons are not suitable. The best way to obtain good colour matching is to use a real flower as a sample to match both crepe paper and the pastel crayons.

Crepe paper   60% stretch crepe in single thickness is best, the texture having a close resemblance to real petals.

Duplex crepe   This is a double thickness crepe, it usually has a pale colour on one side with a deeper colour on the other. White duplex crepe is white on *both* sides. A good range of duplex crepe may be obtained from Paper Chase, 213, Tottenham Court Road, London W1. There is a material list at the head of each flower instructions, these give further information regarding crepe paper, etc.

Paper tissues   Throughout the book, paper tissues are often mentioned. These are very useful for padding stems, etc. The tissues need not be of best quality, in fact the cheaper multi-coloured ones are best as they are not so thick. To cut into strips, remove a tissue from the box and fold it in half lengthwise; strips may then be cut across, usually about $\frac{1}{2}$ in wide unless otherwise stated.

Tissue paper   May well be confused with above! Old tissue which has been used as packing is best for daffodil sheath and crocus, etc. For sweet peas, best acid free tissue is used, a wide range of lovely colours being available.

Newspaper   Plain unprinted newspaper can be obtained from a newspaper printing works. If this is not possible, a cheap quality child's drawing book will do. Look at the plain edge of your newspaper to see the type of paper. This paper is used when making the leaves of some of the flowers.

Textured wallpaper   Anaglypta, or textured white wallpaper, is used for the primula leaves. This can be purchased from a wallpaper shop or DIY supermarket.

A section of textured white anaglypta wallpaper

SPECIAL TECHNIQUES

To transform flat crepe paper into a beautiful flower, which looks exactly like a real one, is a great source of satisfaction! Various techniques are used to create the rounded shapes and delicate curves. Practise first on an odd piece of crepe paper to get 'the feel' of how to do it.

The first essential is that you understand the grain and stretch of crepe paper. Throughout the book you will often see the term 'running from top to bottom' this is to describe the stretch lines (or grain) which run from the top to the bottom of each fold. *See Fig 1.1, A & B.*

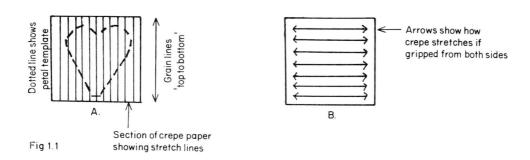

Fig 1.1

When cutting out petals the template is always laid on a section of crepe with the grain running from top to bottom, as shown in *Fig 1.1A.* When cutting a strip for covering stems, etc. turn the paper, as in *Fig 1.2,* and cut right across the whole fold to the required width.

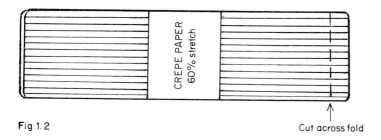

Fig 1.2

Bowling or cupping

To produce a bowl shape, e.g. for anemones, roses, etc. grip the petal either side with the thumbs in front and fingers behind and stretch gently outwards. The thumbs are placed where the 'bowl' is required, e.g. either at the base or near the top of the petal. *See Fig 1.3.*

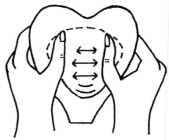

Fig 1.3

14

Frilling

Gently stretch the top edge of the petal to give a frilly edge. *See Fig 1.4.*

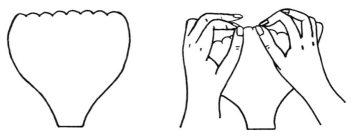

Fig 1.4

Curling

Place the edge of a ruler behind the petal with the thumb in front, gently stroke the paper on the underside up to the top edge. *See Fig 1.5.*

Speedy fringe snipping

Fold a strip of crepe of the required width and snip the top edge all the way along. Then unfold it and the strip looks like a cake frill. When sticking a fringe round the centre of a flower, always roll it round evenly and make sure plenty of glue is used to prevent it slipping down. *See Fig 1.6.*

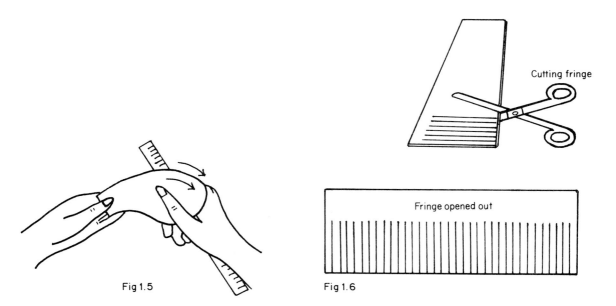

Cutting fringe

Fringe opened out

Fig 1.5

Fig 1.6

Sticking two layers of crepe

Always use the glue sparingly when sticking two layers of crepe together, otherwise it soaks through and ruins it. Do not do large sections of paper at one time — a small area at a time is best. Cut a section of crepe of a suitable size, then fold it in half, making a good crease at the folded edge. Open the section out, and using the spatula proceed to spread the glue sparingly, with the grain of the paper. When you have covered about a 1 in width, bring the other half over and, commencing from the fold, smooth from left to right to get all the air out. Press only lightly when doing this and use the fingertips. Fold the top layer back again and spread glue on the next 1 in width, then bring it over onto the glued area again and smooth as before. Continue doing 1 in widths until the whole section is glued together. Then press it under a book until it is quite dry and nice and flat. *See Fig 1.7.*

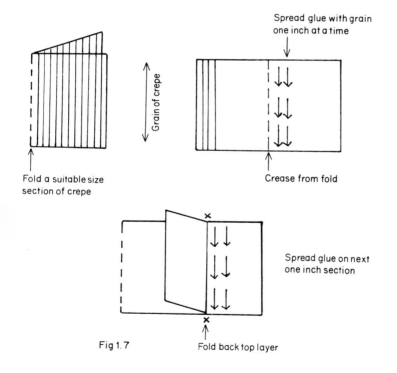

Fig 1.7

Other information

When cutting petals from *single* crepe, if you fold the crepe over several times you can then cut several petals at one time.

When cutting the 'V's' at the top of a calyx, fold the calyx shape in half, then in quarters and cut the 'V's' out. Open it out again and you will see you have found a quicker way of doing it!

Waxing

Waxing instructions are given with the water lily. I have only waxed the water lily up to now as doing the same with any of the other flowers makes them look like plastic and, therefore, they are not so realistic. The water lily is a waxy looking flower and, therefore, more suited to this treatment.

Winding rose wires

To cover a rose wire with a strip of crepe requires a little practice. First of all the strip of crepe should only be about $\frac{1}{4}$ in wide; crepe which is too wide produces very thick and lumpily wound wire!

Put a little glue on the end of the crepe paper strip, and attach it to the top of the wire. Grasp the top of the wire firmly between the first finger and thumb of your right hand and, using the left hand to guide the strip down the wire, proceed to twirl the wire around, all the time pressing very firmly with the finger and thumb of the right hand. A little glue may be added, but if the crepe is wound tightly very little glue is needed, just a spot at the top, in the middle, and at the bottom.

If the crepe becomes loose as you proceed down the wire, continue to the bottom then grasp the top in one hand and the bottom in the other and re-twist to tighten the loose areas. Please note: when cutting up the covered rose wire into the stamens or the pistil always put a small blob of glue on the cut end otherwise it may come undone! With a little practice the art of covering a rose wire is soon acquired.

Padding with paper tissues

Fold a paper tissue in half lengthwise and cut it into $\frac{1}{2}$ in wide strips. Each strip is then opened out. Using plenty of glue the strip is wound round the stem wire to pad it out. When 'bumps' and rounded shapes are required, the strip is twisted as it is wound round. If sufficient glue is used, the required shape may be moulded with the finger tips.

Final suggestion

It is recommended that the reader commences by making a simple flower to begin with. The anemone has been especially designed for this purpose as it is very easy to make. The results being very colourful and effective.

Having mastered the anemone, the reader is then more experienced in handling the crepe paper and will approach with confidence their next choice.

The accuracy of pattern templates is *very important*. When the patterns have been traced onto card and cut out, check they are correct by laying them on top of the original pattern and making sure they fit exactly.

The parts of a flower

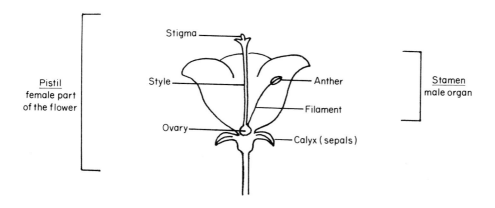

Location of various parts of a flower

2. *Anemone*

This anemone has been especially designed for the beginner in the art of Paper Flower Sculpture. It is very simple and, therefore, ideal to give the reader confidence in the handling of crepe paper.

Anemone flowers are cup or bowl-shaped, the leaves are borne on the stem in whorls of three.

Materials

Black crepe paper and various shades of mauve – red, purple, mauve-pink – for the flowers and leaf-green for the leaves
Green plastic-covered garden wire, 2 mm thick for the stems
12-inch ruler
Adhesive (Latex-type)
2 pairs of sharp scissors – one large and one small
Pliers for cutting wire
Tracing paper
Thin card for templates
Lead pencil (B)

ANEMONE FLOWER

Cut a length of stem wire 8 in long, cover the top two inches with a strip of black crepe cut from across the fold, width about $\frac{1}{4}$ in. Wind round the wire and secure with spots of glue. Bend the covered wire over to form a small hook $\frac{1}{2}$ in depth. *See Fig 2.1.* Squeeze the hook together. Cut two strips of black crepe paper:

1. $\frac{1}{2}$ in × 6 in
2. $\frac{3}{4}$ in × 6 in

Fold each strip in turn and fringe the top edge as shown *Fig 2.2.*

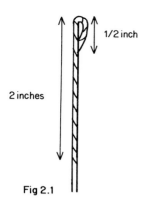

1/2 inch

2 inches

Fig 2.1

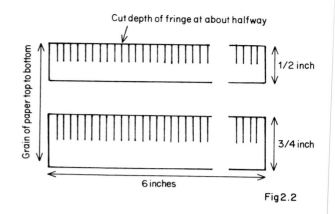

Grain of paper top to bottom

Cut depth of fringe at about halfway

1/2 inch

3/4 inch

6 inches

Fig 2.2

Cover the hook at the top of the stem wire with glue, take strip 1 and place the top of the hook at the base of the fringe. Proceed to wind it round and round, adding frequent spots of glue and keeping the top edge even. Wind strip 2 round in the same way, placing the first fringe top at the base of the second fringe. *See Fig 2.3 & 2.4*.

Finally, wind a further narrow strip of black crepe at the base of the completed centre, as shown *Fig 2.4*. Secure with glue to make sure the two fringes are firmly attached to the stem.

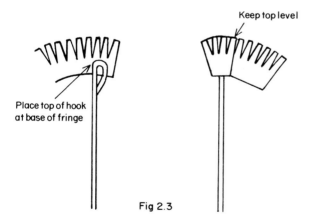

Keep top level

Place top of hook at base of fringe

Fig 2.3

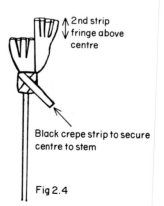

2nd strip fringe above centre

Black crepe strip to secure centre to stem

Fig 2.4

When the centre has been completed, press out the second fringe. The centre of the anemone is now ready for the petals.

Cut eight petals from single red crepe paper (or any of the other colours). The petal pattern is given in *Fig 2.5*.

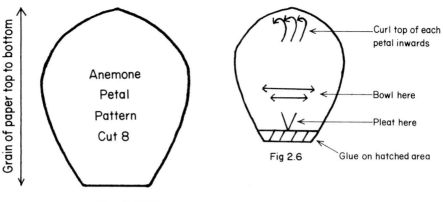

Fig. 2.5 **Pattern**

Take the first petal and bowl and curl as shown *Fig 2.6*. Make a small pleat at the base, spread glue on the hatched area also shown *Fig 2.6*. Affix the petal to the centre as in *Fig 2.7*.

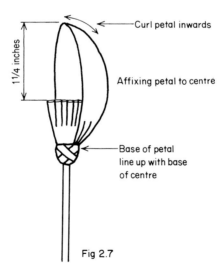

Proceed fixing the petals in the same way, making sure they are all at the same level. Four are evenly spaced round the centre first, and the remaining four are placed between the joins of the inner petals.

Cut a strip of leaf-green crepe about ½ in width and, commencing at the base of the flower, wind down the stem to within about 1 in of the bottom (the 1 in which is left uncovered at the bottom, is useful because it enables the flower to be pushed into oasis when displaying it. If the stem is covered with crepe all the way down, you are not able to do this. Of course the crepe must be terminated several inches higher if the oasis is wet!)

Continue by winding the strip back up the stem, adding spots of glue to hold; terminate under the flower head.

ANEMONE LEAVES

The leaf pattern is given in *Fig 2.8.* The leaves are best made using double crepe. So first of all glue sections of crepe together to the approximate leaf size. *See Fig 2.9.* (Refer to Chapter 1, under Special Techniques, for how to glue two layers of crepe together.)

Lay the leaf pattern on the double section of crepe and cut it out. Fringe the leaf by cutting down the lines as shown in *Fig 2.10.*

Curl the leaf outwards using the ruler. Prepare the remaining five leaves in the same way and affix three directly below the flower head, and the other three about 2 in lower down the stem. Paint glue on the hatched area as shown in *Fig 2.10* and stick to the flower stem. *See Fig 2.11.* for the completed anemone.

Anemone Leaf Pattern Cut 6

Fig. 2.8 Pattern

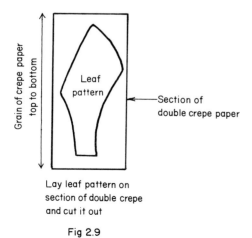

Grain of crepe paper top to bottom

Leaf pattern

Section of double crepe paper

Lay leaf pattern on section of double crepe and cut it out

Fig 2.9

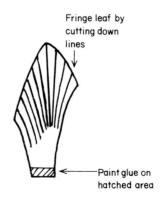

Fringe leaf by cutting down lines

Paint glue on hatched area

Fig 2.10

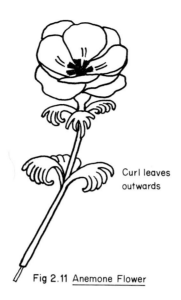

Curl leaves
outwards

Fig 2.11 <u>Anemone Flower</u>

ANEMONE BUD

To make the anemone bud, paint a minute amount of glue along bottom inside edge of the assembled flower and draw the petals together. *See Fig 2.12.*

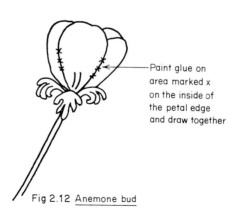

Paint glue on
area marked x
on the inside of
the petal edge
and draw together

Fig 2.12 <u>Anemone bud</u>

3. Crocus

Crocuses are simple flowers to make, arranged in a flower pot or bowl containing real bulb fibre, they are very realistic and colourful. (Refer to the final chapter, Useful Ideas for Display and Storage, for how to prepare the flower pot, etc.)

Materials

Purple crocus   Purple orange and deep yellow crepe paper for the flowers
Leaf green crepe for the leaves
Crumpled white tissue paper for the sheath
Adhesive (Latex-type)
Small sharp scissors
12-inch ruler
Lead pencil (B)
Tracing paper
Thin card for templates
Green plastic-covered wire, 2 mm thick for stems
White pastel crayon
Pliers for bending and cutting wire

White crocus   White duplex (e.g. double crepe paper)
Yellow and leaf-green pastel crayons
Centre of flower and leaves, same as above

White crocus with pale mauve stripe
Use white duplex crepe
Colour with pale mauve pastel crayon

Yellow Crocus   Yellow crepe paper
Leaf-green pastel crayon

PURPLE CROCUS FLOWER

Cut a length of 2 mm plastic covered wire approximately 4½ in long. Cover the top 2 in with a ¼ in wide strip of orange crepe, wind from the top of the wire down adding spots of glue to hold, then wind from the bottom back up to the top, thus giving a double covering of crepe. Take a section of orange crepe, 1 in wide × 2 in deep. *See Fig 3.1.* The grain of crepe should run from top to bottom. Fringe the top edge to a depth of ¼ in.

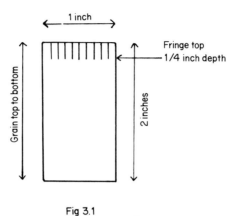

Fig 3.1

Cover the top 1¾ in of the stem wire with glue and lay on the section of orange crepe with the top of the wire at the base of the fringe. *See Fig 3.2.* Using spots of glue along the whole length, proceed to roll it up, keeping the top fringe even. *See Fig 3.3.*

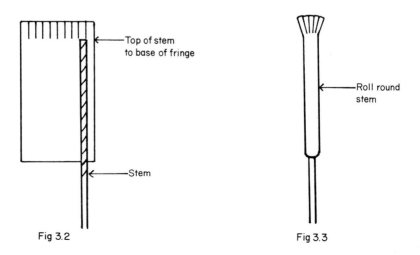

Fig 3.2

Fig 3.3

Cut three stamens from the deep yellow crepe paper with the grain top to bottom as before. The pattern for stamens is shown in *Fig 3.4*. Paint a small amount of glue along the folded edge and affix the first stamen. The top is placed $\frac{1}{4}$ in below the top of the fringe (which is the stigma). *See Fig 3.5.* The remaining two are evenly spaced round the stem of the stigma. Draw the bottom edge of each one together with a small spot of glue.

For the petals of all crocuses it is best to use double crepe, therefore for the purple and the yellow it will be necessary to glue some sections of crepe together. (Refer to Chapter 1, under Special Techniques, for how to glue two layers of crepe together.) Prepare six sections to the approximate size of the petal pattern in *Fig 3.6*.

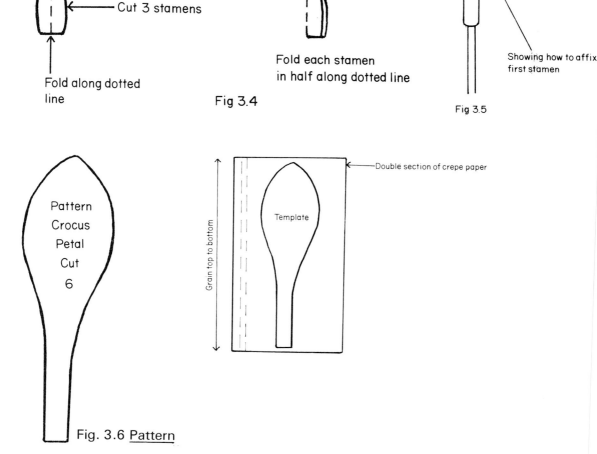

Pattern

Cut 3 stamens

Fold along dotted line

Fold each stamen in half along dotted line

Fig 3.4

1/4 inch

Spot of glue and draw edges together

Showing how to affix first stamen

Fig 3.5

Pattern
Crocus
Petal
Cut
6

Grain top to bottom

Template

Double section of crepe paper

Fig. 3.6 <u>Pattern</u>

Having cut the six petals from the double sections of crepe, proceed to prepare for affixing. Each petal is shaded using the pastel crayon, white is used for the purple crocus. *See Fig 3.7* for areas to shade, and *Fig 3.8* for how to bowl and curl each one.

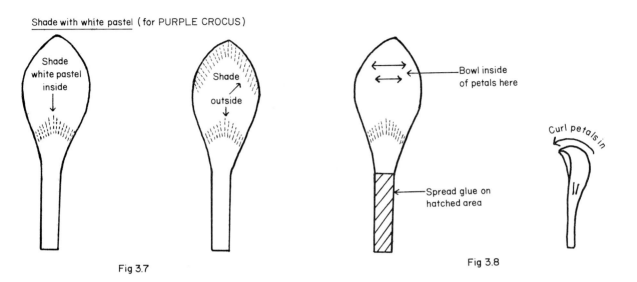

Shade with white pastel (for PURPLE CROCUS)

Shade white pastel inside

Shade outside

Bowl inside of petals here

Spread glue on hatched area

Curl petals in

Fig 3.7

Fig 3.8

Spread glue on the hatched area shown in *Fig 3.8* and affix the first three petals which should be evenly spaced and all level at the tops. *See Fig 3.9*.

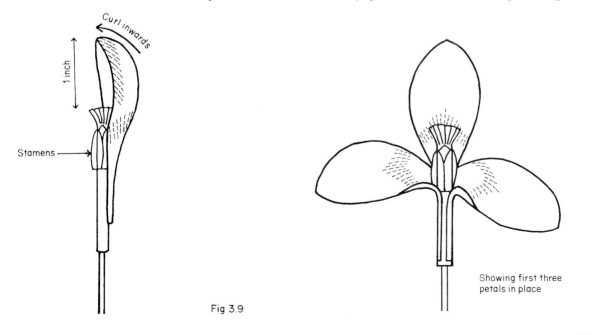

Curl inwards

1 inch

Stamens

Fig 3.9

Showing first three petals in place

The remaining three petals are placed between the spaces of the first three, taking care to keep them all at the same level; the tip of each petal should be about 1 in above the tip of the fringed stigma, as shown in *Fig 3.9*.

When making a bowl of assorted crocuses, it is best to have the flowers at various stages of opening.

CROCUS BUD

To make the flower into a bud, paint a very little glue along the inside bottom edge of each petal, and gradually draw the petals together, working right round the flower and securing all the petals. *See Fig 3.10.* Likewise, a semi-open crocus can also be made by not drawing in so much. Finally, a full-blown flower is made by not painting any glue at the base of petals, just leaving it open as it is when you have just completed affixing all six petals.

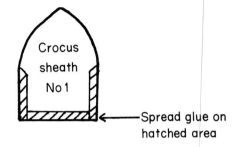

Crocus sheath No 1

Spread glue on hatched area

Fig 3.11 Pattern

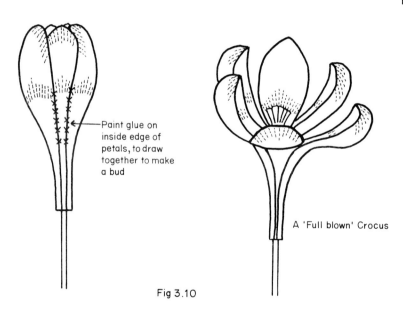

Paint glue on inside edge of petals, to draw together to make a bud

A 'Full blown' Crocus

Fig 3.10

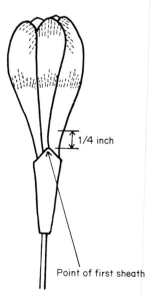

1/4 inch

Point of first sheath

Fig 3.12

Cut the first sheath pattern given in *Fig 3.11*, using white crumpled tissue paper. Placing the glue round the outer edge of the sheath (the hatched area shown in *Fig 3.11*) wrap it round the stem of the flower with the point $\frac{1}{4}$ in below the base of the petals, *see Fig 3.12*. Cover the stem below the sheath with a strip of leaf-green crepe paper wound round and secured with glue. Terminate 1 in up from the bottom.

CROCUS LEAVES

Glue a section of double leaf-green crepe paper together for the leaves, size about 4 in deep × 3 in wide. (It is a good idea to press this under a book to give a nice flat finish). *See Fig 3.13.* The size of leaf is given in *Fig 3.14.*

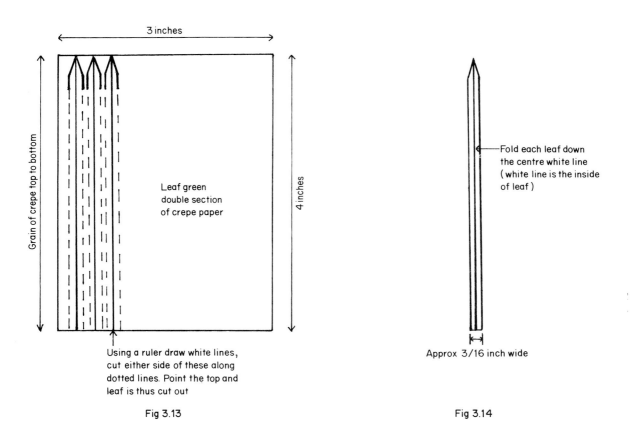

3 inches

Grain of crepe top to bottom

Leaf green
double section
of crepe paper

4 inches

Using a ruler draw white lines, cut either side of these along dotted lines. Point the top and leaf is thus cut out

Fig 3.13

Fold each leaf down the centre white line (white line is the inside of leaf)

Approx 3/16 inch wide

Fig 3.14

When the section of leaf-green crepe paper is quite dry, using a white pastel crayon and a ruler, draw white lines approximately $\frac{1}{4}$ in apart right across the section of paper. *See Fig 3.13.* All that now remains is to cut the leaves out, each one approximately $\frac{3}{16}$ in wide. Shape the tops to a good point. Each leaf is then folded lengthwise along the centre white line. With the white line on the inside, paint a spot of glue on the base of each leaf. Affix five or six round the stem, each leaf varying slightly in height, e.g. the tips just above the top of the flower. Cut sheath No 2, as given in *Fig 3.15,* from crumpled tissue paper (white) as before. The second sheath is wrapped round on top of the leaves (like wrapping a bunch of flowers) with the point about ½ in *lower* than the sheath No 1 point and on the otherside of the stem. *See Fig 3.16* for completed crocus.

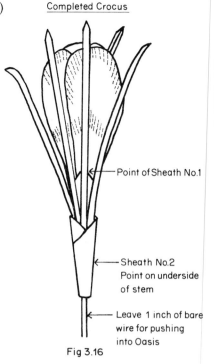

Completed Crocus

— Point of Sheath No.1

— Sheath No.2
Point on underside
of stem

— Leave 1 inch of bare
wire for pushing
into Oasis

Fig 3.16

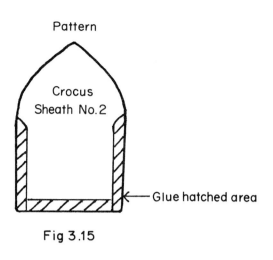

Pattern

Crocus
Sheath No.2

— Glue hatched area

Fig 3.15

Fig 3.17 shows how to colour the petals of the white with mauve stripe duplex crocus. Refer to *Fig 3.18* for the pure white crocus, and *Fig 3.19* for the yellow crocus.

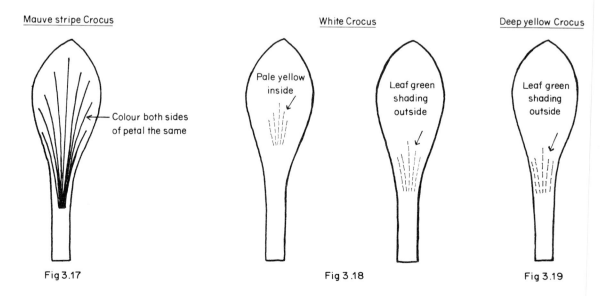

Mauve stripe Crocus

— Colour both sides
of petal the same

Fig 3.17

White Crocus

Pale yellow
inside

Leaf green
shading
outside

Fig 3.18

Deep yellow Crocus

Leaf green
shading
outside

Fig 3.19

4. Daffodil

The daffodil has a cup or 'trumpet', within which are six stamens and the stigma. Six petals surround the trumpet. There are a wide variety of colours and colour combinations. The flower with the shorter trumpet or cup is the narcissus, and the longer trumpet variety is the daffodil.

Materials

For making a daffodil with a deep yellow trumpet and paler yellow petals:

Deep yellow single crepe paper for the trumpet and a shade of paler yellow for the petals

Leaf-green single crepe for leaves and stem

Thin pale green card for leaves and trumpet shaper

Paper tissues for padding

Adhesive (Latex-type)

2 pairs of sharp scissors, one large and one small

Green plastic-covered garden wire 2 mm thick for stems

12-inch ruler

Pliers for cutting wire

Thin card for templates

Tracing paper

Lead pencil (B)

A section of crumpled off-white tissue paper for the sheath

Leaf-green pastel crayon for the flower, and a white pastel crayon for the leaves

DAFFODIL FLOWER

Cut a stem wire approximately 13 in long. Cover the top 2 in with a $\frac{1}{4}$ in wide strip of deep yellow crepe, wound round and secured with spots of glue. Bend the top of the covered wire over to form a $\frac{1}{2}$ in hook. *See Fig 4.1.*

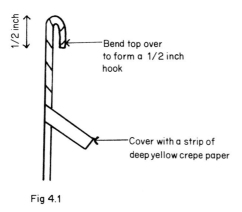

Bend top over
to form a 1/2 inch
hook

Cover with a strip of
deep yellow crepe paper

1/2 inch

Fig 4.1

With grain of paper running from top to bottom, cut a piece of deep yellow crepe $\frac{1}{2}$ in wide × 2 in deep. Roll it up to form a small stick, secure the outer edge with a small amount of glue. Bend the top of the 'stick' over and make a very small blob on the end, use a tiny spot of glue to hold. This is the stigma. *See Fig 4.2.* Place the stigma so as it stands 1 in above the top of the stem hook; thread the bottom half of it through the hook and wind round the stem, securing with glue. *See Fig 4.2.*

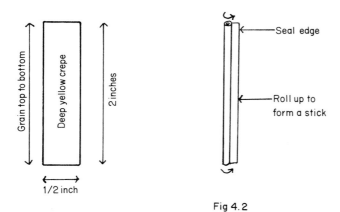

Grain top to bottom

Deep yellow crepe

2 inches

1/2 inch

Seal edge

Roll up to
form a stick

Fig 4.2

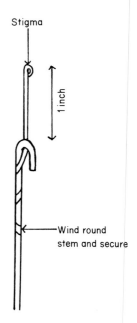

Stigma

1 inch

Wind round
stem and secure

Rhododendron clusters wired to real leaves.

Anemones displayed with fresh foliage (broom).

Daffodils, narcissi, primulas all with paper leaves, also a paper ivy trail.

Crocuses in a wheelbarrow filled with dry bulb fibre.

Roses with paper leaves.

Sweet peas displayed with glycerined fern.

Water lily with paper leaves.

Pinks (white and purple edged eye) displayed with glycerined butcher's broom.

African daisies with dried gypsophila.

Pinks with paper leaves.

Carnations with buds and paper leaves, also a paper variegated ivy trail.

Cut three further pieces of deep yellow crepe, each ½ in wide × 2 in deep as before. Roll each section up and form three sticks. Secure the outer edge of all with glue.

Lay the three sticks in a row, and put a spot of glue in the centre of each one, then pick them up and thread them up from the bottom of the stem hook, so as they are arranged either side of the stigma. These are the stamens. Put another spot of glue at the base of each set of three and stick them to the stem hook so that they stand upright. Trim the tops of the six stamens so as they are level and just below the stigma. *See Fig 4.3.* Put a spot of glue on the tips you have cut.

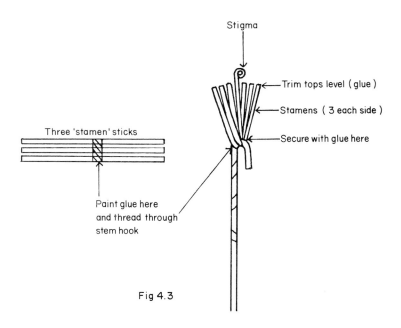

Fig 4.3

Having completed the stamens and stigma, the hook may now be squeezed together.

The trumpet is cut from deep yellow double crepe. Prepare a section of crepe in advance to give time for the glue to dry before cutting the trumpet out. *See Fig 4.4* for the trumpet pattern. To prepare the double crepe, spread glue on one inch at a time as explained under Special Techniques in Chapter 1.

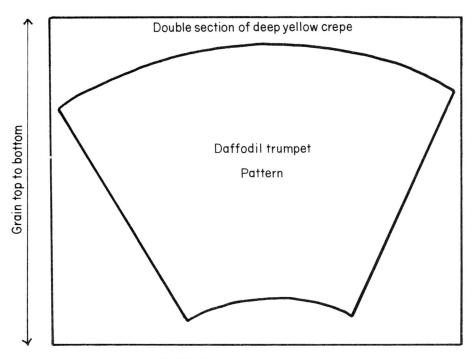

Daffodil pattern above actual size

Fig 4.4

When the trumpet has been cut out, fold it in half, then in quarters, finally in eighths. Draw the 'm' at the top and cut it out, thus giving the frilled top as shown in *Fig 4.5*.

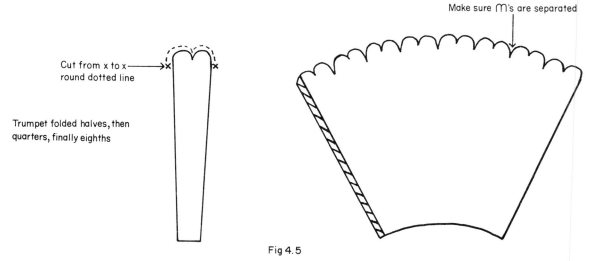

Make sure m's are separated

Cut from x to x—round dotted line

Trumpet folded halves, then quarters, finally eighths

Fig 4.5

Spread glue along the hatched edge (*Fig 4.5*) and join to the opposite side forming a trumpet. Gently stretch the top and curl over using a ruler. Cut a trumpet shaper from thin card, as in the pattern given in *Fig 4.6*. Glue the shaper together, and push it down inside the prepared trumpet. It will be a tight fit, and you will have to gently force it inside. *See Fig 4.7*. The shaper is left in the trumpet until the petals have been affixed as this gives the flower a good shape at the base. It is also used when the daffodils are packed away in boxes as it keeps them in good shape and prevents crushing.

Pattern

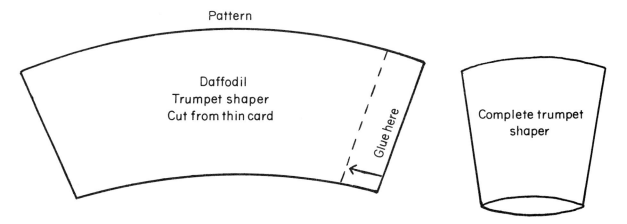

Daffodil
Trumpet shaper
Cut from thin card

Glue here

Complete trumpet
shaper

Fig 4.6 Daffodil trumpet shaper

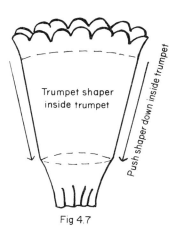

Trumpet shaper
inside trumpet

Push shaper down inside trumpet

Fig 4.7

The trumpet is now ready to be glued in place on the stem. Spread a very narrow line of glue all round the bottom inside edge of the trumpet and thread the stem through from the top. Affix the trumpet base $\frac{1}{4}$ in below the base of the stem hook. *See Fig 4.8.* Gather it in and secure.

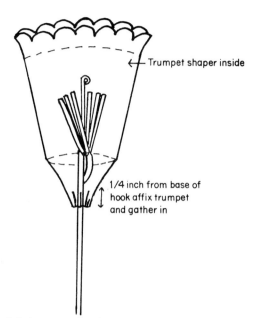

Trumpet shaper inside

1/4 inch from base of hook affix trumpet and gather in

Fig 4.8 <u>A cross section showing how to affix Daffodil trumpet</u>

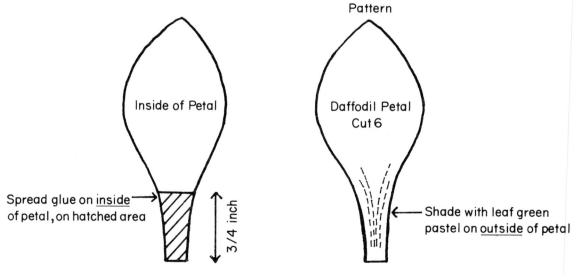

Inside of Petal

Spread glue on <u>inside</u> of petal, on hatched area

3/4 inch

Pattern

Daffodil Petal Cut 6

Shade with leaf green pastel on <u>outside</u> of petal

Fig 4.9

Cut six petals from pattern, *see Fig 4.9*, using the pale yellow crepe in single thickness.

Colour the outside of each petal as shown in *Fig 4.9* with a leaf-green pastel crayon. Apply glue to the hatched area also shown *Fig 4.9* and affix the first petal, the tip of which should be level with the tip of the trumpet. Mark at the place where the bottom of the petal comes on the stem, using a ballpoint pen. It is easier then to keep the other petals at the same level. *See Fig 4.10*. Affix three evenly spaced ones around first, and the remaining three in the spaces.

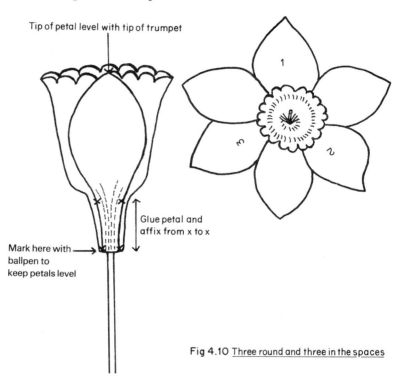

Tip of petal level with tip of trumpet

Glue petal and affix from x to x

Mark here with ballpen to keep petals level

Fig 4.10 Three round and three in the spaces

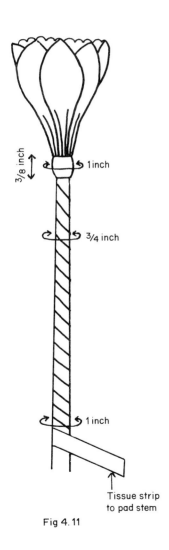

3/8 inch

1 inch

3/4 inch

1 inch

Tissue strip to pad stem

Fig 4.11

When all six petals are in place, remove the trumpet shaper. Cut several strips of paper tissue $\frac{1}{2}$ in wide, and commencing at the base of the petals, proceed to twist and wind the strips round, adding glue to hold, continue until a small bump is formed 1 in in circumference. *See Fig 4.11*. Cover this bump with a $\frac{1}{2}$ in wide strip of leaf-green crepe paper, wound round and secured with glue. When the bump has been covered, using more strips of paper tissue pad the stem, beginning directly below the bump. Continue winding the strips round the stem, using a liberal amount of glue. The top of the stem should be about $\frac{3}{4}$ in in circumference, graduating to 1 in round the bottom of the stem.

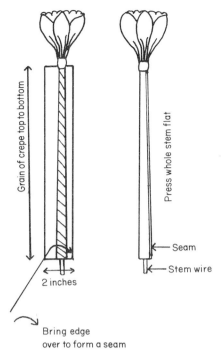

Grain of crepe top to bottom

Press whole stem flat

Seam

Stem wire

2 inches

Bring edge
over to form a seam

Fig 4.12

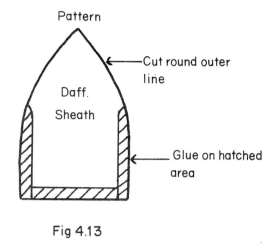

Pattern

Cut round outer
line

Daff.
Sheath

Glue on hatched
area

Fig 4.13

To cover the stem, cut a piece of leaf-green crepe about 2 in wide (grain top to bottom). Completely cover the padded stem with glue and lay it on the strip of green. Draw the two edges together to form a seam down one side of the stem. When the glue is dry, trim off the excess, and finally flatten the whole length of the stem between your finger and thumb. *See Fig 4.12*. If you wish to use the daffodils in oasis, leave about 1 in of the stem wire uncovered.

Now, bend the flower head over and cut a sheath from the crumpled off-white tissue paper. The sheath pattern is given in *Fig 4.13*.

Paint the glue on the hatched area of the sheath and wrap it round the stem. The bottom edge of the sheath should be 1 in below the base of the bump. *See Fig 4.14*.

DAFFODIL LEAVES

The daffodil leaves are cut from pale green, thin card, and covered with leaf-green crepe paper. Cut a card leaf from the pattern given in *Fig 4.15*, also cut a section of leaf-green crepe about 1 in wide, with grain running

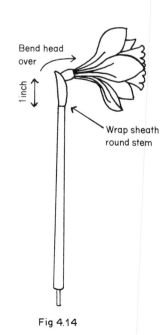

Bend head
over

1 inch

Wrap sheath
round stem

Fig 4.14

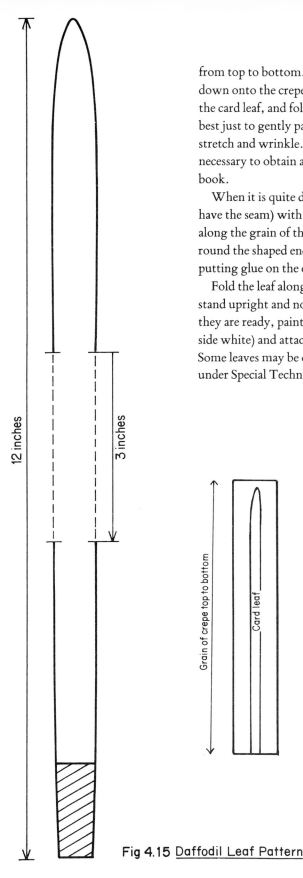

from top to bottom. Cover one side of the card leaf with glue and stick it down onto the crepe in the centre. Paint more glue on the other side of the card leaf, and fold the two edges of the crepe towards the centre. It is best just to gently pat the crepe onto the glued card leaf otherwise it will stretch and wrinkle. Trim off any excess crepe, and add a little glue where necessary to obtain a neat finish. The leaf can then be pressed under a book.

When it is quite dry and flat, colour one side (the side which does not have the seam) with a little white pastel crayon, working from the base along the grain of the crepe. To finish off the tip of the leaf, cut the crepe round the shaped end, fold it back a little, trim off the card leaf tip before putting glue on the crepe and sealing the end.

Fold the leaf along the centre, all the way up to the end, this makes it stand upright and not flop. Each flower needs at least two leaves. When they are ready, paint a small amount of glue on the bottom inch (coloured side white) and attach to the base of the daffodil stem, one on either side. Some leaves may be curled at tips if required. *See Fig 1.5* in Chapter 1 under Special Techniques.

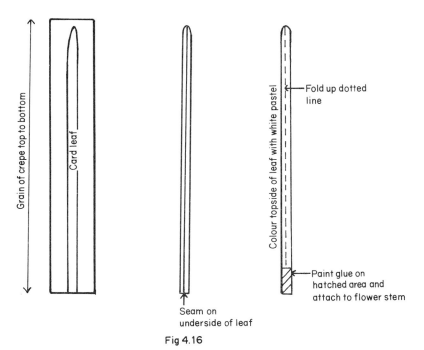

Fig 4.16

Fig 4.15 Daffodil Leaf Pattern

DAFFODIL BUD

A daffodil bud is very simple to make, cut a 13 in stem wire (2 mm) as for the flower, and cover the top 3 in with a $\frac{1}{4}$ in wide strip of pale yellow crepe. Bend the top over to form a 1 in hook; do not close the hook. Cut some tissue strips, and using a good amount of glue proceed to wind and twist the tissue strips round the hook. The shape of the bud is shown in *Fig 4.18*. The depth of the padding should be about $1\frac{1}{2}$ in, and the centre circumference approximately $1\frac{1}{2}$ in also. If you use enough glue you will be able to mould the bud into shape with your fingers. Cut three pale yellow crepe daffodil petals from the pattern, cut about $\frac{3}{4}$ in off the petal base. The prepared bud is then covered with glue and the petals are wrapped round one at a time, making sure the whole of the padding is covered. A couple of slightly loose edges on the last petal look very realistic, as if the bud is just opening out.

The bump is then formed directly below the base of the bud petals and covered with a strip of the same leaf-green crepe as for the flower. The bud stem is made up like the flower stem. The sheath should be cut from crumpled tissue paper as for flower but larger, e.g. about $2\frac{1}{4}$ in from tip to base, and at least $1\frac{1}{2}$ in wide. When the bump and stem have been completed, wrap the sheath round the bud. The base of this is placed $\frac{1}{2}$ in below the bottom of the bump. A little leaf-green pastel may be applied to the base of the bud if desired. Partially opened daffodil buds are made by making a flower in the normal way, and smoothing the outer petals down onto the trumpet.

Fig 4.17 Completed Daffodil

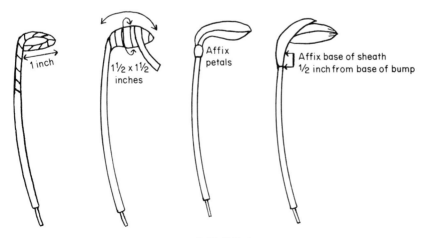

1 inch

$1\frac{1}{2}$ x $1\frac{1}{2}$ inches

Affix petals

Affix base of sheath $\frac{1}{2}$ inch from base of bump

Fig 4.18 Daffodil Bud

5. Narcissus

5 NARCISSUS

This flower has pure white petals, with a bright yellow centre edged with red.

Materials

White and bright yellow crepe paper for the flowers
Leaf-green crepe paper for the stem and leaves
Red and emerald green felt-tip pens
Pale-green paper tissue for the centre of the flower
Paper tissues for padding stem, etc.
Thin pale green card for leaves
Green plastic covered wire 2 mm thick
Adhesive (Latex-type)
2 pairs of sharp scissors – one large and one small
12-inch ruler
Lead pencil (B)
Pliers for bending and cutting wire
Pastel crayons in pale yellow and white
Small section of off-white crumpled tissue paper for the sheath
Tracing paper
Thin card for templates

NARCISSUS FLOWER

Cut a length of stem wire approximately 13 in long, cover the top $1\frac{1}{2}$ in with a $\frac{1}{4}$ in wide strip of yellow crepe paper. Wind round and secure with spots of glue. Bend the wire over to form a $\frac{1}{2}$ in hook. Cut a further piece of yellow crepe, with grain running from top to bottom, size 1 in square. *See Fig 5.1*. Cut this section in half along the grain line, and roll each piece up to form a stick, sealing the edge of each with a little glue.

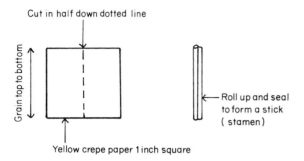

Cut in half down dotted line

Grain top to bottom

Yellow crepe paper 1 inch square

Roll up and seal to form a stick (stamen)

Fig 5.1

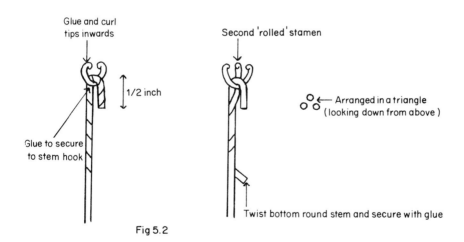

Glue and curl tips inwards

1/2 inch

Glue to secure to stem hook

Second 'rolled' stamen

Arranged in a triangle (looking down from above)

Twist bottom round stem and secure with glue

Fig 5.2

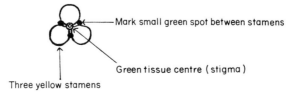

Mark small green spot between stamens

Green tissue centre (stigma)

Three yellow stamens

Fig 5.3 View from above showing centre of Narcissus

These two sticks are the stamens, and are affixed to the stem hook as follows: take the first one and put a small spot of glue in the centre of it, thread the stamens up from the bottom of the hook and secure the glued area onto the top underside of same. *See Fig 5.2.* Add a further small amount of glue to the two ends and roll each one in towards the centre as shown *Fig 5.2.* Another stamen is threaded through the hook, but one only is rolled in at the top, the other half is twisted round the stem and glued down. *See Fig 5.2.* There are now three stamens each with its tip rolled towards the centre forming a triangle shape when viewed from above. Take a pale green paper tissue and cut a small section approximately 1 in × $\frac{1}{2}$ in, and roll tightly between finger and thumb to form a stick shape. Paint glue on the bottom $\frac{1}{8}$ in and insert same between the three stamens, squeeze the rolled stamens to grip the tissue stick, trim it off so as it is level with the stamens. Using the green felt-tip pen, mark a small spot between each stamen as shown *Fig 5.3.*

Cut a section of yellow crepe $\frac{1}{2}$ in deep × $2\frac{1}{2}$ in wide, *see Fig 5.4*, with the grain of paper top to bottom. Colour along the top edge with a red felt-tip pen; only a very narrow band of red is required. Glue the hatched edge and fix the two edges together to form a cylindrical shape. *See Fig 5.4.* Stretch and frill the red top edge. Close the stem hook by squeezing with the pliers. Spread glue round the bottom inside edge of the cylinder to a depth of about $^3/_{16}$ in, thread the stem with the stamens at the top, down through the cylinder and position the red top edge approximately $\frac{1}{8}$ in above the top of the stamens. Gather in and secure to the stem wire. *See Fig 5.5.*

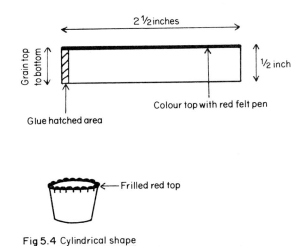

Fig 5.4 <u>Cylindrical shape</u>

Fig 5.5 <u>Cross section showing frilled centre in place</u>

Fig 5.6 Pattern

Cut six petals from white crepe paper as in *Fig 5.6*. Colour one side of each petal with a fan of pale yellow pastel. *See Fig 5.7*. (The fan of yellow is on the inside of the petals). Measure from the tip of the first petal to a depth of $1\frac{1}{8}$ in and mark with a very small pencil dot. Pleat, and spread glue on the hatched area. *See Fig 5.7*. Line up the top of frilled cylinder centre with pencil dot and affix to stem. Mark around the stem with felt pen at the base of the first petal; remaining petals may then be lined up at the base to keep them level. Three are evenly spaced around and three in the spaces.

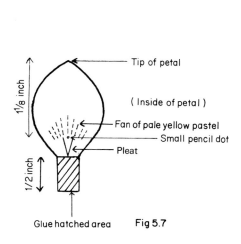

Fig 5.7

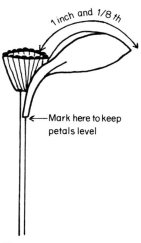

Fig 5.8 Placing of first petal

When all six petals have been affixed, separate each one by pinching together at the base. See *Fig 5.13*. Cut several paper tissue strips about ½ in wide and proceed to pad the stem. Commencing from the base of the petals, wind the tissue strips round the stem adding frequent spots of glue. To form the 'bump' as shown in *Fig 5.9*, wind and twist the strip. If enough glue is used you are able to mould the bump to the correct shape with your fingers.

The bump size should be 1 in round the centre, smoothed on either side, with the depth about ½ in as in *Fig 5.9*.

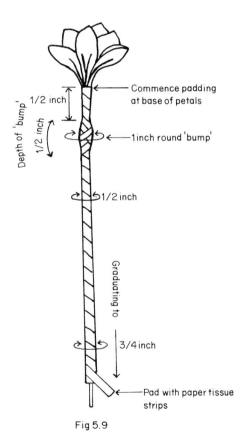

Fig 5.9

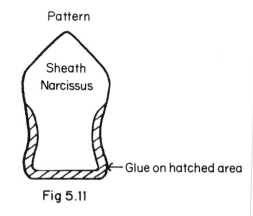

Pattern

Sheath
Narcissus

Glue on hatched area

Fig 5.11

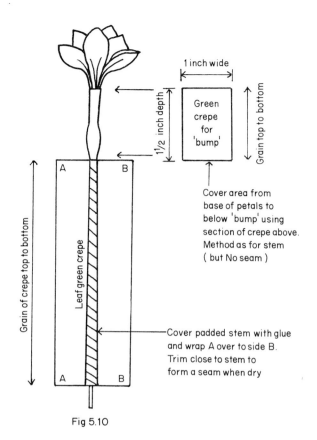

1 inch wide

Green crepe for 'bump'

1/2 inch depth

Grain top to bottom

A   B

Leaf green crepe

Grain of crepe top to bottom

A   B

Cover area from base of petals to below 'bump' using section of crepe above. Method as for stem (but No seam)

Cover padded stem with glue and wrap A over to side B. Trim close to stem to form a seam when dry

Fig 5.10

Continue padding the stem with paper tissue strips until it measures a $\frac{1}{2}$ in circumference at the top, graduating to $\frac{3}{4}$ in at the bottom as shown in *Fig 5.9.* To cover the stem use leaf-green crepe. Cut a piece of leaf-green crepe, with the grain running top to bottom, approximate size 1 in wide × $1\frac{1}{2}$ in deep. This section is used to cover the area from the base of flower head to below the bump. *See Fig 5.10.* Paint glue over the bump, etc. and wrap first one side of the crepe over and stick down, then bring the other side over and stick it so as the whole of the paper tissue is covered. Trim off the excess crepe. There is no seam here, just a neat, smooth covering of green. *See Fig 5.10.* Cut a further piece of leaf-green crepe, with the grain running top to bottom, size 1 in wider all round the stem. Cover the whole of the padded stem with glue, lay the stem onto the crepe, and bring edge A over to edge B. Seal to form a seam all down one side. When dry, trim the seam as close to the stem as possible. Flatten and smooth the length of the covered stem and bend the flower head over, commencing the bend just below the bump.

Cut the sheath from the pattern given in *Fig 5.11*. Use crumpled off-white tissue paper for this.

Paint a little glue along the hatched edge of the crumpled tissue sheath, and wrap round the flower stem – the point of this being at the base of the bump. When the flower is completed, bow the stem a little. *See Fig 5.12.*

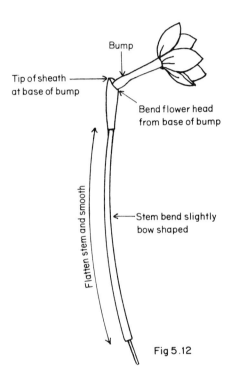

Bump

Tip of sheath
at base of bump

Bend flower head
from base of bump

Flatten stem and smooth

Stem bend slightly
bow shaped

Fig 5.12

NARCISSUS LEAVES

Cut the leaves from thin pale green card. The pattern is given in *Fig 5.13*. The card leaf is then covered with glue on one side and stuck down onto a piece of leaf-green crepe which has been cut about 1 in wide and approximately ½ in longer than the card leaf. The grain of crepe must run from top to bottom. *See Fig 5.14*. Trim the crepe so it will just meet in the centre of the card leaf. Cover the other side of the card leaf with glue and bring the two edges of crepe together so that they meet and completely cover the card leaf. To shape the top of the leaf, fold the crepe back a little from the tip, trim off the card leaf tip and cut the crepe to a good pointed shape; then re-seal the top. When the leaf is dry, colour one side only with a *little* white pastel (the side without the seam is best). Smooth the pastel into the crepe with finger tips. There should be no lines of white showing, but instead a silvery colour all over the leaf. Fold the completed leaf down the centre with the white on the inside of the fold. Paint a little glue on the bottom 1 in (white side) and attach to the bottom of the flower stem. Make as many leaves as possible with a minimum of two per narcissus. Attach the second leaf on the opposite side of the stem. Some leaves may be curled with the edge of a ruler, if required. *See Fig 1.5*, under Special Techniques in Chapter 1.

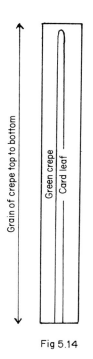

Fig 5.14

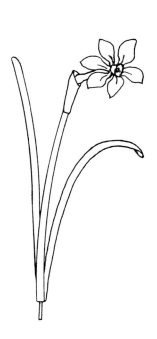

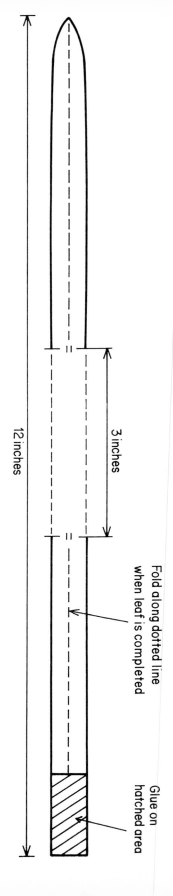

48

NARCISSUS BUD

Cut a 14 in length of 2 mm thick stem wire, cover the top 2 in with a $\frac{1}{4}$ in wide strip of white crepe paper, wind round and secure with glue. Bend the covered area over and form a $\frac{1}{2}$ in hook, but do not close this.

Cut several $\frac{1}{2}$ in wide strips of paper tissue and pad to a bud shape by winding and twisting round the hook. Use plenty of glue, the shape of the bud may then be moulded. Continue the padding down the whole stem, forming a bump $2\frac{1}{4}$ in from the bud tip. The bump and the stem are the same measurements as for the flower, and are covered in the same way. Leave the stem covering of leaf green until the bud is completed. *See Fig 5.15*, for the size and shape of the bud. *Fig 5.16* shows the completed bud. Cut four petals from white crepe paper. *See pattern Fig 5.6.* Paint glue round the edges and on the bottom tab, wrap each petal round the padded bud until it is covered.

Glue a separate section of leaf-green crepe around the bump, etc., the same as for the flower; cover the stem, and affix sheath. Bend over as shown in *Fig 5.16*. Colour a little leaf-green pastel at base of bud petals.

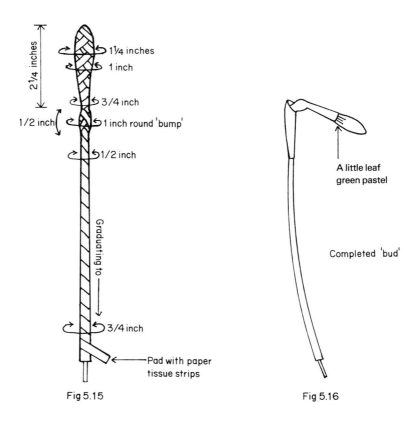

Fig 5.15

Fig 5.16

6. Primula

This is a primrose-like flower which grows in a wide variety of beautiful colours, the leaves are obovate, mid-green.

Materials

Yellow crepe paper for stigmas
Purple crepe for the flowers (or yellow, red, pink, etc., in fact almost any colour!)
Leaf-green crepe for leaves and stems
Stiff white paper (*not* card, typing paper will do)
Felt-tip pens in dark orange (*not* bright orange) and yellow
Pastel crayons in pale green and dark red
Adhesive (Latex-type)
Sharp-pointed scissors
Small pliers
12-inch ruler
Lead pencil (B)
Matchstick
Paper tissues
Rose wires
Tracing paper
Thin card for templates

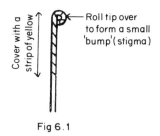

Fig 6.1

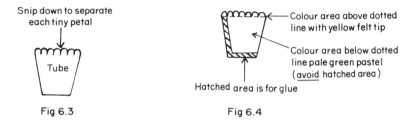

Fig 6.2 <u>Pattern</u>

PRIMULA FLOWER

Take a rose wire and cover the top 1 in with a $\frac{1}{4}$ in wide strip of yellow crepe paper; wind round the wire and secure with spots of glue. Roll the tip of the covered wire over to form a small 'bump' (this is called the stigma) *See Fig 6.1*. Using the stiff white paper, cut out the centre tube which will enclose the stigma. *See Fig 6.2* for the actual size of the pattern.

Cut the top of the tube very carefully, snip down as shown to separate each of the tiny petals. *See Fig 6.3*. Colour the top of the tube above the dotted line with the yellow felt-tip pen. *See Fig 6.4*. The area below the dotted line is coloured pale green, using the pastel crayon. Do not colour right to the edge of the tube as the glue has to be applied here later and it will not stick if it has crayon on it.

Fig 6.3

Fig 6.4

Using a matchstick, roll the tube round it with the green and yellow colours on the inside. *See Fig 6.5*. Spread glue only along the side edge (*not* along the bottom edge). Seal, making the shape as shown in *Fig 6.5*. The tube should be tight at the bottom edge, but not so tight at the top. Withdraw the match by pulling from the top.

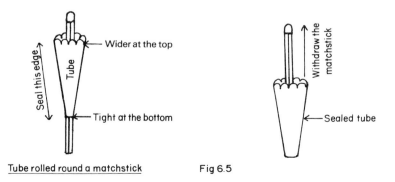

<u>Tube rolled round a matchstick</u>   Fig 6.5

Threading from the top, draw the prepared stem (with the stigma on the top) through the tube, positioning the stigma just level with the top of the green-coloured area inside. *See Fig 6.6.* Mark the stem with a pencil at the place where the base of the tube comes. Withdraw the stem and proceed to thicken the area just above the pencil mark by winding a $\frac{1}{4}$ in wide strip of yellow crepe around it and securing with glue. Thicken the area so that it fits tightly when threaded down through the tube again. Paint a little glue over the padded area and squeeze the tube base around it and secure. *See Fig 6.7.*

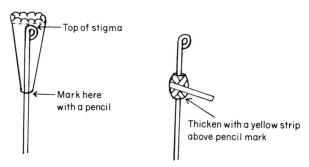

Top of stigma

Mark here with a pencil

Thicken with a yellow strip above pencil mark

Fig 6.6 Cross section showing position of stigma

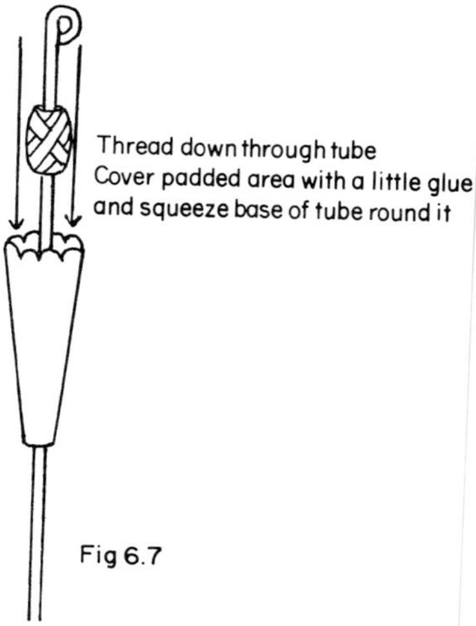

Thread down through tube
Cover padded area with a little glue and squeeze base of tube round it

Fig 6.7

Cut out the 'eye' or centre of the flower, as given in *Fig 6.8*, using white paper. Colour the whole of one side with the yellow felt-tip pen. When dry, colour a little with an orange felt-tip pen on top of the yellow colour as shown in *Fig 6.9*.

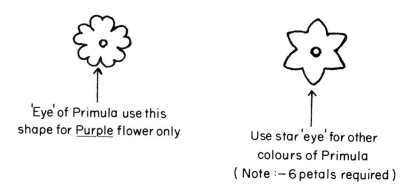

'Eye' of Primula use this shape for <u>Purple</u> flower only

Use star 'eye' for other colours of Primula
(Note :— 6 petals required)

Fig 6.8 Patterns

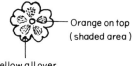

Orange on top
(shaded area)

Yellow all over

Fig 6.9 Colouring of 'eye'
(same for star shape)

Fig 6.8 shows a flower-shaped centre and a star-shaped centre; the flower shape is only used when making a purple primula. All other colours are used on the star-shaped centre. The colouring is the same for both as shown in *Fig 6.9*.

Snip round centre
to enlarge hole

Fig 6.10

Having cut out and coloured the flower centre with the yellow and the orange felt pens, push the point of the small, sharp scissors through the middle, and enlarge the tiny hole enough by snipping all round it, *see Fig 6.10*, to enable the centre to be threaded up from the bottom of the stem (with the tube already fixed at the top). Ease the central hole of the 'eye' over the base of the tube, and gradually wriggle it up to the top of the tube until it is just below the yellow petals. Paint a little glue on the underside of these petals and turn them back and stick them down onto the centre of the 'eye'. *See Fig 6.11*.

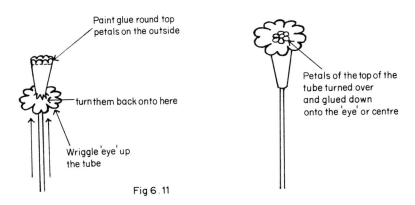

Paint glue round top
petals on the outside

turn them back onto here

Wriggle 'eye' up
the tube

Fig 6.11

Petals of the top of the
tube turned over
and glued down
onto the 'eye' or centre

The centre of the primula is now complete, and ready for the flower petals. The petals can be cut from double or single crepe, it depends on the quality of the crepe you are using. If it is thin and double paper is required, stick sections together, grain top to bottom, and leave to dry before using.

There are five petals for the purple flower, and six petals for the star-shaped eye which is used for all the other colours. The petal pattern is given in *Fig 6.12*. Having cut out the petals, spread glue on the bottom hatched area, make a small pleat at the base and affix the petal to the underside of one of the petals of the 'eye' or centre, *see Fig 6.13*. The bottom $\frac{1}{8}$ in of the petal is stuck to the top of the tube.

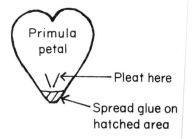

Fig 6.12 <u>Pattern</u>

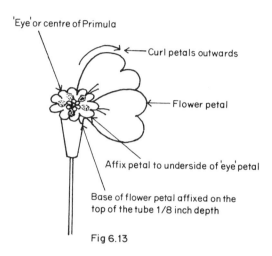

Fig 6.13

Continue affixing the petals until they are all in place. It is simple to position each one, as the petal on the 'eye' comes in the centre of the flower petal each time. When they are all on, lift the 'eye' petals each in turn and spread a little glue on the underside and stick them down firmly onto the flower petals. Cover the stem of the primula with a $\frac{1}{4}$ in wide strip of leaf-green crepe. Commence winding from the bottom of the flower stem and work your way up to the top, terminating under the flower head (at the top of the tube).

Cut the calyx pattern given in *Fig 6.14*, using single leaf-green crepe. Colour the outside of the calyx using the pale-green pastel crayon. Spread glue on the outer edge of three sides of the calyx, (the top edge is not glued), and wrap it round beneath the flowerhead. The base of the calyx comes just below the base of the tube. To complete the flower, colour the stem in dark red pastel crayon for purple flowers and all dark colours, and pale green for yellow flowers and other pale colours.

Fig 6.14 <u>Pattern</u>

PRIMULA BUD

To make a primula bud, just make a flower in the normal way and squeeze the whole flower head together with the finger tips. For a smaller bud, take a rose wire and cover the stem with a $\frac{1}{4}$ in wide leaf-green strip. Make a small $\frac{1}{4}$ in hook at the top. Cut out about three petals of single crepe, cut them a little smaller all round. Paint a small amount of glue at the base of each petal and roll them round the hook at the top of the stem. Cut a calyx and colour as for the flower, and wrap it round the 'bud'. *See Fig 6.15*. To complete the flowers and prepare them for assembling into a plant, curl each petal outwards using the edge of the ruler, also cut small pieces out round the edges of the petals to give them a slightly frilled look. For assembling *see Figs 6.22 and 6.23* in the primula leaves section.

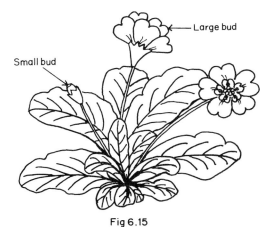

Fig 6.15

PRIMULA LEAVES

Materials

Embossed white wallpaper (anaglypta)
Leaf green crepe
Rose wires
Adhesive (Latex-type)
Sharp scissors
12-inch ruler
Pale green pastel, white pastel and dark red
Tracing paper and thin card for templates
Lead pencil (B)

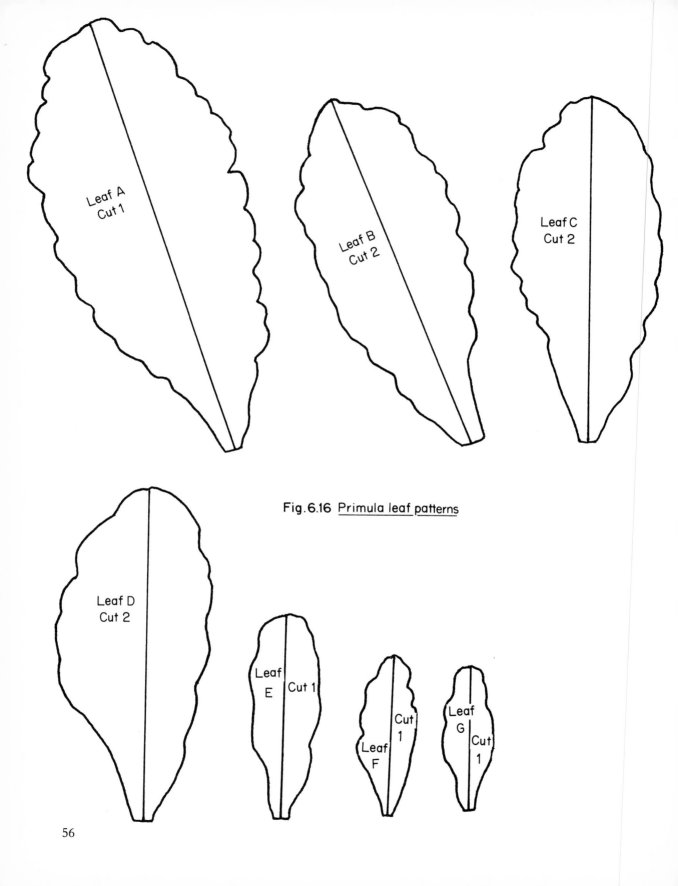

Leaf A
Cut 1

Leaf B
Cut 2

Leaf C
Cut 2

Fig.6.16 Primula leaf patterns

Leaf D
Cut 2

Leaf
E   Cut 1

Leaf
F   Cut 1

Leaf
G   Cut 1

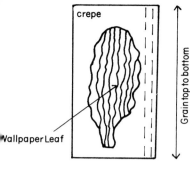

crepe

Grain top to bottom

Wallpaper Leaf

Fig. 6.17

Cut the ten leaves from the patterns given in *Fig 6.16*. Make cardboard templates. Lay each template onto a section of wallpaper. (The embossed lines of the paper should be vertical). It is easier if a ballpoint pen is used to trace round the outline of each leaf before cutting out. Cover seven rose wires with a narrow strip of leaf-green crepe, securing at intervals with spots of glue. Leaves E, F and G do not need a wire.

Each leaf is made up as follows: spread glue all over the *right* side of the first leaf, making sure it is in all the crevices of the wallpaper. Massage with the fingertip after the adhesive has been applied. Apply sparingly, otherwise it will soak through the crepe and spoil the surface. Lay the glue side face down onto a section of leaf-green crepe, with the grain of paper top to bottom. *See Fig 6.17*. Press the crepe into the crevices so that the design of the wallpaper shows through. Trim the crepe so as there is approximately a $\frac{1}{4}$-in border all round the leaf. *See Fig 6.18*. Snip all round the edge with sharp scissors, as shown also in *Fig 6.18*.

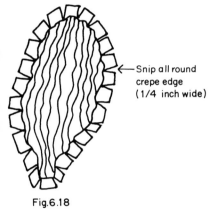

← Snip all round crepe edge (1/4 inch wide)

Fig.6.18

Proceed to glue each flap of crepe down onto the back of the leaf. Paint the glue on the wrong side of the leaf and massage into crevices as before, making sure the glue is also spread well round the outer edge. Lay the glue side face down onto another section of leaf-green crepe as before. Smooth down well to bring the design through. When dry, trim the excess paper round the edge, taking care not to cut into the first covering of crepe. *See Fig 6.19* and *Fig 6.20*.

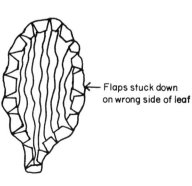

← Flaps stuck down on wrong side of leaf

Fig.6.19

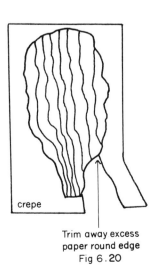

crepe

Trim away excess paper round edge
Fig 6.20

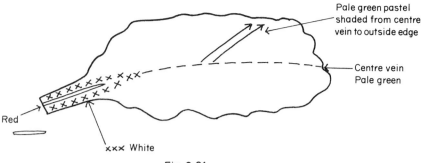

Fig.6.21

Glue the covered rose wire down the centre back of the wrong side of the leaf. When dry, colour as shown in *Fig 6.21*.

The remaining leaves are made in the same way. Please note: leaves E, F and G have a heavier colouring of pale green as they are young leaves. Bend the outer edges of each leaf over, using the edge of a ruler.

To assemble: gather the prepared bunch of primula flowers, paint a small spot of glue on the bottom of leaves E, F and G, and stick them round (about half way down) the stems of the flowers. *See Fig 6.22.*

The remaining leaves are assembled, according to size, around the outside of the bunch shown in *Fig 6.23*. A small spot of glue may be applied at the base of some of these where necessary to make them appear to be growing from a central point. Finally, bind the whole plant with a strip of leaf-green crepe to hold all the stems together. *See Fig 6.23.*

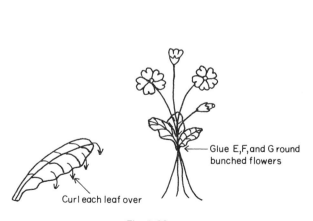

Fig.6.22

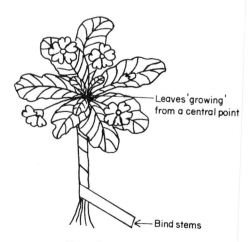

Fig.6.23

58

7. Single Pink

Pinks have been famous since Classical times for their beauty and for their scent. This is the single pink with white and purple-edged eye. The grey-green foliage is attractive in winter.

Materials

Crepe paper in pale mauve-pink, white and leaf green
Fine plastic-covered wire $1\frac{1}{4}$ mm thick, and rose wires
Paper tissues
White pastel crayon
White poster colour
Purple poster colour or felt-tip pen in the same colour
Fine paint brush
Adhesive (Latex-type)
Small, sharp scissors
Pliers
12-inch ruler
Thin card for templates
Tracing paper
Lead pencil (B)

SINGLE PINK FLOWER

Cut a length of fine plastic-covered wire of $1\frac{1}{4}$ mm thickness, (approximately 8 in). Cover the top 1 in with a strip of white crepe paper $\frac{1}{4}$ in wide. Wind round and secure with spots of adhesive top and bottom. Bend the top over using the pliers and form a $\frac{1}{4}$ in hook. *See Fig 7.1*. Cover a rose wire in the same way, using a $\frac{1}{4}$ in wide strip of white crepe as before. Cut $1\frac{1}{2}$ in off this wire, and save the remainder for future flowers. Thread this length of wire through the stem loop, and twist it round twice at the base. Paint a small spot of glue on the two ends where it has been cut to make sure it does not come undone. To complete the centre, bend the two stamens as shown in *Fig 7.2*, and squeeze the hook together.

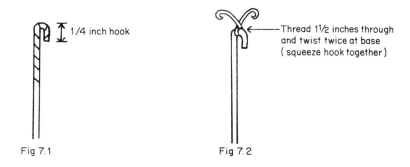

1/4 inch hook

Thread 1½ inches through and twist twice at base (squeeze hook together)

Fig 7.1   Fig 7. 2

Cut five petals from the pale mauve-pink crepe-paper pattern given in *Fig 7.3*. (Double crepe gives a good result, to do this glue two sections of the crepe together). However, single crepe may be used if desired.

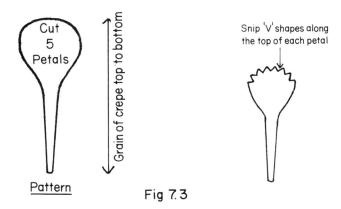

Cut 5 Petals

Grain of crepe top to bottom

Snip 'V' shapes along the top of each petal

Pattern

Fig 7.3

Snip 'v' shapes along the top of each petal and, using the white poster colour, paint the bottom half of the petals as shown in *Fig 7.4*. A narrow fan of purple is then added along the top edge of the white. When using the poster paint, use the *minimum* of water.

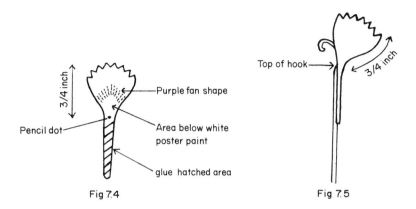

Fig 7.4

Fig 7.5

Measure $\frac{3}{4}$ in from the top of the petal down, and mark with a small pencil dot, see *Fig 7.4*. Spread the glue on the hatched area, and affix to the top of the prepared stem, lining up the pencil dot with the top of the stem hook. *See Fig 7.5*. The remaining four petals are affixed at the same level, making sure that the purple fans join up and make a circle round the centre of the flower.

Cut $\frac{1}{2}$ in wide strips of paper tissue and, commencing 1 in below the top of the petals, wind and twist round, using spots of glue, until the area beneath the flower head is padded, ready to receive the calyx. *See Fig 7.6.* for measurements, etc.

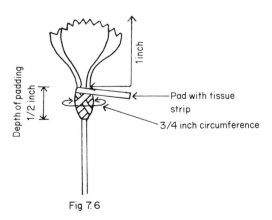

Fig 7.6

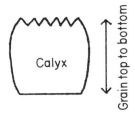

Fig 7.7 Pattern

Glue together a section of leaf-green double crepe paper and cut a calyx. Colour this one side with the white pastel. The pattern for the calyx is given in *Fig 7.7*. Paint glue round the inside of the calyx (white colouring goes on the outside) and wrap this round the padded area. Line up the base of the calyx with the base of the padding. *See Fig 7.8.*

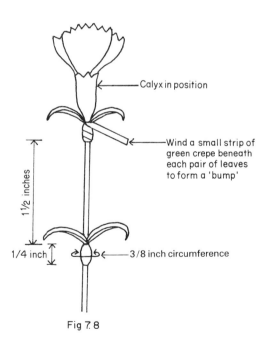

Fig 7.8

Using a $\frac{1}{4}$ in wide strip of leaf-green crepe, commence winding from the *bottom* of the stem upwards; use spots of glue at regular intervals. Winding in this way gives a smoother finish; terminate at the base of the calyx.

SINGLE PINK LEAVES

Cut two leaves from each size. The patterns are given in *Fig 7.9*. Use leaf-green double crepe paper as before. Colour each leaf both sides with white pastel crayon; curl outwards using edge of a ruler. Affix in pairs, the small ones directly under the calyx, size 2 about $1\frac{1}{2}$ in down the stem, and size 3 about 2 in lower still. Using the $\frac{1}{4}$ in wide leaf-green strip, wind and twist directly beneath each leaf pair to form a small bump. Complete by colouring the stem and the bumps with the white pastel. *See Fig 7.10* for the completed flower.

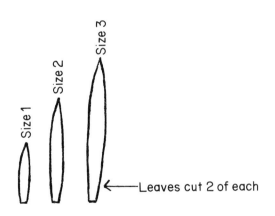

Size 1

Size 2

Size 3

← Leaves cut 2 of each

Fig 7.9 Patterns

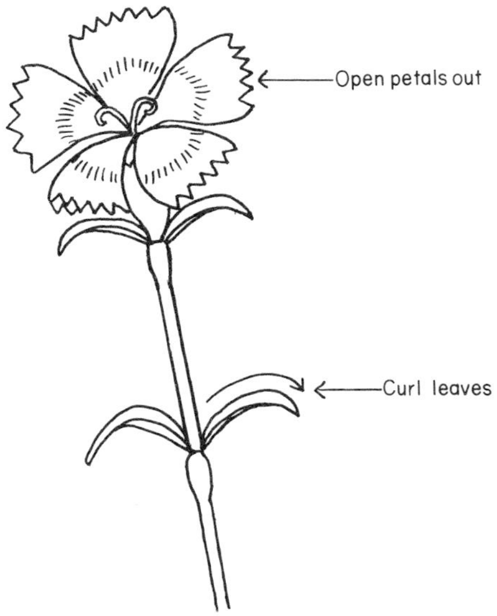

—— Open petals out

←—— Curl leaves

Fig 7.10 Completed flower

8. Old-fashioned Pink and Carnation

Both pinks and carnations come in a variety of colours, with fringed edges to the petals. The leaves are pointed and grey-green in colour.

Materials

Pale pink, white, and pale mauve-pink single crepe paper for the pinks
Red, white, pink, and pale yellow for the carnations
Leaf-green crepe for leaves and stems
Green plastic-covered stem wire 2 mm thick
Paper tissues for padding
White pastel crayon
Adhesive (Latex-type)
2 pairs of sharp scissors – one large and one small
Pliers for bending and cutting wire
12-inch ruler
Thin card for templates
Tracing paper
Lead pencil (B)

OLD-FASHIONED PINK FLOWER

Cut a stem wire approximately 8 in long and cover the top 2 in with a
¼ in wide strip of the same colour crepe as the flower to be made. Wind
the strip round the wire and secure with spots of glue. Bend the top of
the wire and form a ½ in hook. Close the hook by squeezing together
with the pliers.

Cut a quantity of petals. The pattern is given in *Fig 8.1*. The best way
to cut a lot of petals is to divide the fold of crepe into two, cutting down
the folded edge. The pattern may then be placed on top of several layers of
crepe paper, and cut out. *See Fig 8.2.* Cut approximately six bundles of
petals, and taking each bundle in turn snip the small 'v' shapes round the
top edge, using the small sharp scissors.

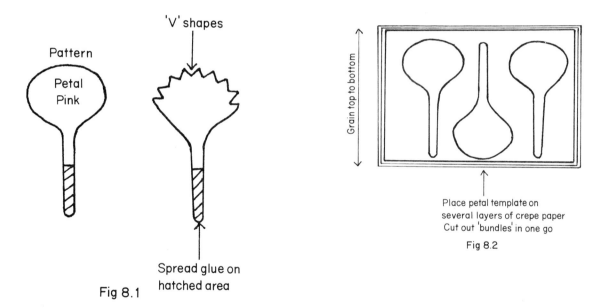

Pattern

Petal
Pink

'V' shapes

Spread glue on
hatched area

Fig 8.1

Grain top to bottom

Place petal template on
several layers of crepe paper
Cut out 'bundles' in one go

Fig 8.2

Divide the petals into groups of three and arrange each group into a fan
shape. Paint a little glue on the hatched area and proceed to affix to the
stem hook, as shown in *Fig 8.3*. Make sure the petals are kept level at the
top, otherwise the centre of the flower will stick up and be entirely the
wrong shape.

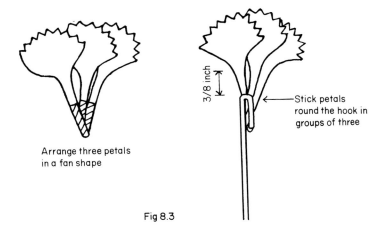

Arrange three petals
in a fan shape

3/8 inch

Stick petals
round the hook in
groups of three

Fig 8.3

Proceed sticking the petals round the hook, each set of three arranged in a fan, before painting the glue on and affixing. When the pink measures approximately $2\frac{1}{2}$ in across the top enough petals have been attached. Make sure the flower has enough petals – they should be well bunched and not sparse and loose.

Cut several $\frac{1}{2}$ in wide strips of paper tissue and, using ample glue, wind and twist around the base of the petals to build up the area in readiness for the calyx. *See Fig 8.4* for dimensions.

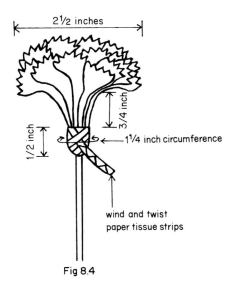

2½ inches

3/4 inch

1/2 inch

1¼ inch circumference

wind and twist
paper tissue strips

Fig 8.4

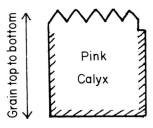

Fig 8.5 <u>Pattern</u>

Prepare a section of leaf-green double crepe paper by glueing two pieces together, of a suitable size for the calyx and the leaves. Cut the calyx from the pattern given in *Fig 8.5*. Colour one side of the calyx with a white pastel crayon, (the white-pastel side being the outside). Smooth the pastel with the finger-tips so as it blends into the crepe. Spread glue round the hatched area, and position the bottom edge of the calyx at the base of the flower petals. Stick down one edge first, then grasp the petals from the top in your left hand and proceed to wrap the calyx round and seal the other edge. *See Fig 8.6*. This will be quite a tight fit, hence it is necessary to grasp the petals. Once the calyx has been secured, tease the petals out again as shown in *Fig 8.7*. Cover the stem using a $\frac{1}{4}$ in wide strip of leaf-green crepe. Wind round the stem commencing about 1 in up from the bottom. Secure with frequent spots of glue, terminating under the calyx.

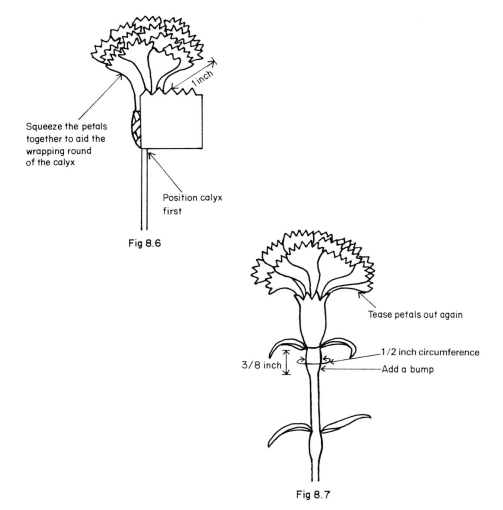

Fig 8.6

Fig 8.7

OLD-FASHIONED PINK LEAVES

Cut six leaves, two of each size from the previously prepared section of leaf-green double crepe paper. Patterns given in *Fig 8.8*.

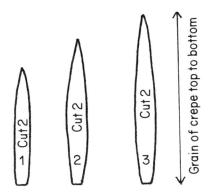

Fig 8.8 Pink Leaf patterns

Each leaf is coloured both sides with the white pastel crayon. Smooth the pastel with finger-tips to blend. The two size 1 leaves are curled at the tips, and a little glue painted at the bottom. Affix one on either side of the stem directly below the calyx as shown in *Fig 8.7*. Size 2 leaves are affixed in the same way, approximately 2 in lower down the stem. Likewise, size 3 leaves are attached $1\frac{1}{2}$ in lower down the stem. Cut a $\frac{1}{4}$ in wide strip of leaf-green crepe and, commencing directly below each pair of leaves in turn, wind and twist the strip to form a small bump. Add frequent spots of glue to hold. *See Fig 8.7*. To complete: colour the stem and the bumps with the white pastel crayon; blend with the finger-tips as before.

CARNATION FLOWER

This is made by the same method as for the pinks but the patterns are naturally larger and there are more petals.

Cut a stem wire 14 in long, in 2 mm thick plastic-covered wire. Cover the top 3 in with a $\frac{1}{4}$ in wide strip of crepe paper. Colour the same as the flower being made. Bend the top of the wire over and form a $\frac{1}{2}$ in hook, then close the hook with pliers. Cut bundles of petals, using the same method as for pinks, only cut at least eight bundles. Cut 'v' shapes out of the top of the petals. The pattern is given in *Fig 8.9*.

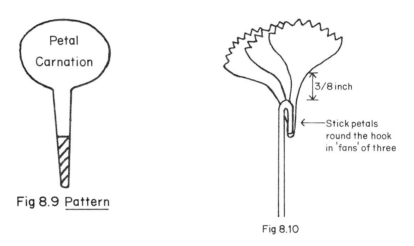

Fig 8.9 <u>Pattern</u>

Petal Carnation

3/8 inch

Stick petals round the hook in 'fans' of three

Fig 8.10

Divide the petals into groups of three as for pinks, and spread glue on the hatched area, then attach to the hook as shown in *Fig 8.10*. Keeping the petals even at the top, continue working round the stem adding groups of three, always arranged in a fan. Plenty of petals are essential for good results as sparse petals make a bedraggled flower. When the carnation measures at least $2\frac{3}{4}$ in across the top and the petals are nice and tightly packed, commence the padded area for the calyx. The pattern is given in *Fig 8.11*.

See Fig 8.12 for the dimensions of padding for the calyx.

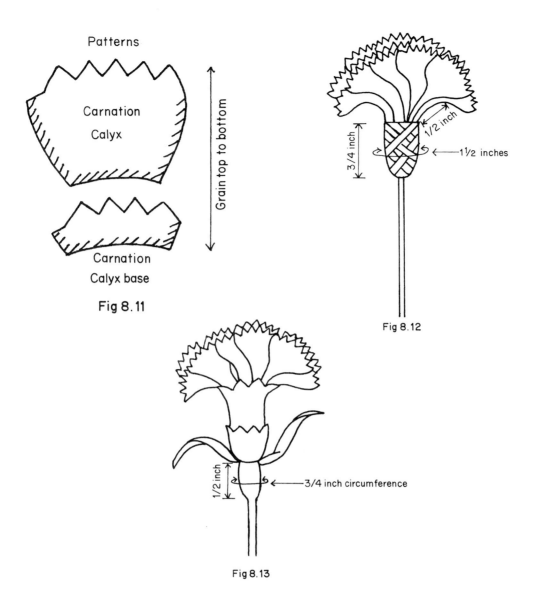

Patterns

Carnation
Calyx

Grain top to bottom

Carnation
Calyx base

Fig 8.11

1/2 inch

3/4 inch

←———1½ inches

Fig 8.12

1/2 inch

←———3/4 inch circumference

Fig 8.13

Prepare a section of leaf-green double crepe paper. There is a calyx and a calyx base, as you will see in *Fig 8.11*. Cut one of each and colour with the white pastel crayon on one side only. (The white pastel going on the outside when affixing). Glue the hatched area of larger calyx first and affix. *See Fig 8.13*. The method is as for pinks. The smaller calyx is glued round on top of the first one at the base. *See Fig 8.13*. Cut a strip of leaf-green crepe paper about $\frac{3}{8}$ in wide and, commencing 1 in up from the bottom of the stem, wind it round securing with spots of glue. Terminate under the calyx.

70

CARNATION LEAVES

Using a further section of leaf-green double crepe, cut six leaves, patterns given in *Fig 8.14*. Colour them both sides with the white pastel and blend with the finger-tips as for pinks. Attach the two smallest leaves as shown in *Fig 8.13*. The second and third pairs are spaced at 2 in intervals down the stem. If a bud is required, do not attach the third pair of leaves, but follow instructions for bud making. With a $\frac{1}{4}$ in wide strip of green crepe, wind and twist to form a small bump beneath each pair of leaves. *See Fig 8.13* for dimensions. Complete by colouring the whole stem and the bumps with the white pastel crayon.

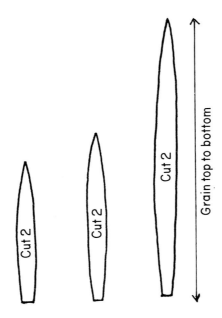

Fig 8.14 Carnation Leaf patterns

CARNATION BUD

A carnation may be made with a bud attached to the flower stem.

Cut a 7 in wire 2 mm thick and cover the top 2 in with a $\frac{1}{4}$ in wide strip of crepe, coloured to match the flower. Make a $\frac{1}{2}$ in hook. Pad the hook with $\frac{1}{2}$ in wide strips of paper tissue. *See Fig 8.15* for dimensions.

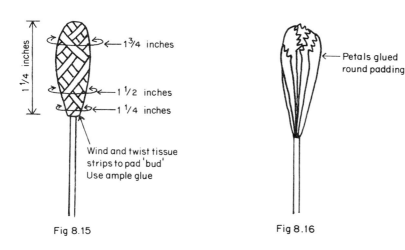

Fig 8.15

Fig 8.16

Wind and twist the tissue paper strips to build up the bud shape. See *Fig 8.15*. Use plenty of glue as it is then possible to mould the padding. Paint glue over the bud and affix approximately six or eight petals, draw the tips in at the top. *See Fig 8.16*. Affix a carnation calyx and calyx base, as shown in *Fig 8.17*, also attach a pair of the smallest leaves plus a bump underneath the same as for the flower. The second pair of leaves are glued approximately $1\frac{1}{2}$ in from the base of the calyx. The bud may then be affixed to the main stem of a specially prepared carnation, e.g. a flower which has only the first two pairs of leaves in place. Using a strip of green crepe $\frac{3}{8}$ in wide, glue and bind the bottom $2\frac{1}{2}$ in of the bud stem on one side of the flower stem. *See Fig 8.18* for position. A pair of the largest leaves are attached at the place where the bud joins the main stem with a bump underneath.

Colour the bud stem, etc. with the white pastel crayon also the area where it has been affixed to the main stem.

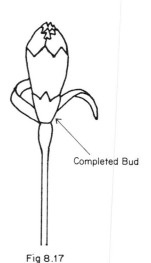

Completed Bud

Fig 8.17

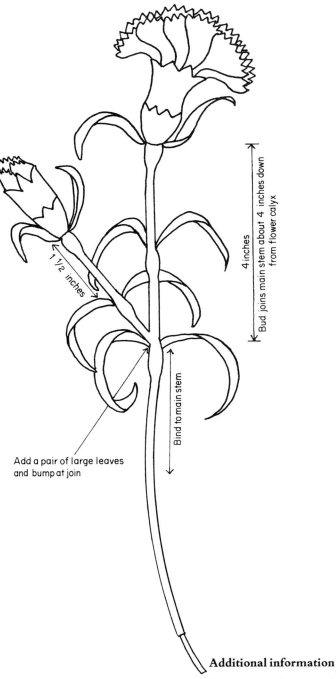

4 inches

Bud joins main stem about 4 inches down from flower calyx

1 1/2 inches

Bind to main stem

Add a pair of large leaves and bump at join

Fig 8.18

Additional information

A very attractive carnation is one named 'Arthur Sim', which is a white flower with red markings on the petal tips. To make one like this is very simple. Using a red felt-tip pen, brush the tops of the petals while they are in bundles before they are separated into fans of three. When the flower is complete, if more red is necessary, bunch the petals together and add more red felt-tip.

9. Rose

The rose has long been the most popular flower; references to its beauty
go far back in history. Originally it blossomed in its natural wildness as a
simple flower with only five petals and from these species the glorious
creations of the present day have evolved.

Materials

Crepe paper: red, yellow or pink according to your own choice of colour
Leaf-green crepe paper
Paper tissues for padding
Green plastic-covered wire for stems, 2 mm thick
12-inch ruler
Adhesive (Latex-type)
Thin card for pattern templates
Tracing paper
Lead pencil (B)
2 pairs of sharp scissors – one large and one small
Pliers
Pastel crayons in wine red and light green
Collection of real rose thorns stored in a matchbox
Clear nail varnish to preserve the thorns

ROSE FLOWER

Cut a stem wire 2 mm thick, length optional, although a long stemmed rose always looks good. Cover the top 3 in with a $\frac{1}{4}$ in wide strip of crepe paper the same colour as the rose to be made. Wind the strip round the wire and secure with spots of glue. Bend the top of the covered wire over and form a $\frac{1}{2}$ in hook. Squeeze the hook together using the pliers. Cut the petals from the patterns given in *Fig 9.1*. Take one petal size A, and covering the stem hook with glue, lay it at an angle onto the petal, as shown in *Fig 9.2*. With the hook $\frac{1}{2}$ in down from the top of the petal, roll the petal round the hook very tightly, making sure that the top of the stem hook does not show. Seal the petal at the base with a little glue. Leave the outer edge of the petal unsealed on the top two thirds so that it rolls back slightly.

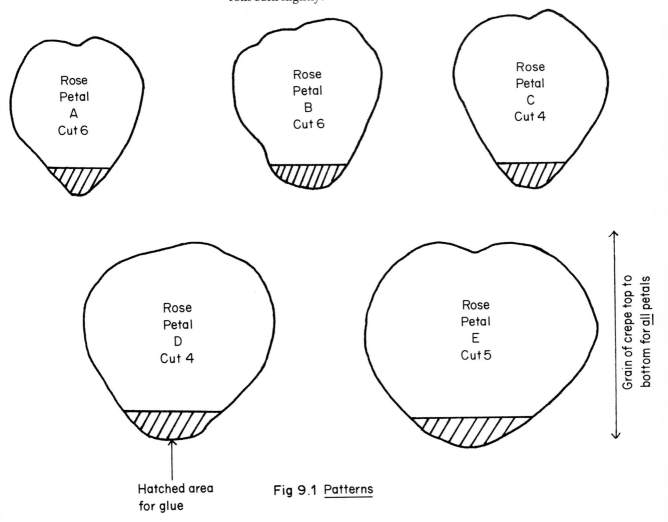

Rose Petal A Cut 6

Rose Petal B Cut 6

Rose Petal C Cut 4

Rose Petal D Cut 4

Rose Petal E Cut 5

Grain of crepe top to bottom for all petals

Hatched area for glue

Fig 9.1 Patterns

Affix a further two size A petals, putting a little glue at the base on the hatched area. Wrap each petal round in turn, positioning the previous rolled edge (join) in the centre of the new petal. Each added petal is $\frac{1}{8}$ in higher than the previous one. *See Fig 9.3.* Curl over the top edge of both petals.

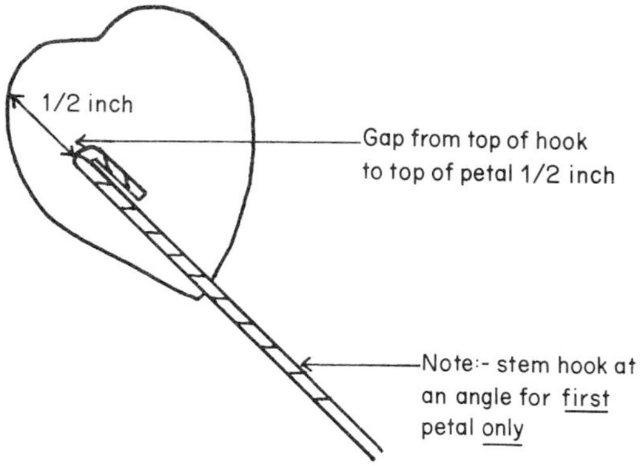

Each added petal 1/8 inch higher

1/2 inch

Gap from top of hook to top of petal 1/2 inch

Note:- stem hook at an angle for <u>first</u> petal <u>only</u>

Rolled first petal A

Curl edge over

Glue and wrap the two edges round, one overlapping the other

Open rolled edge is on the underside

Fig 9.2

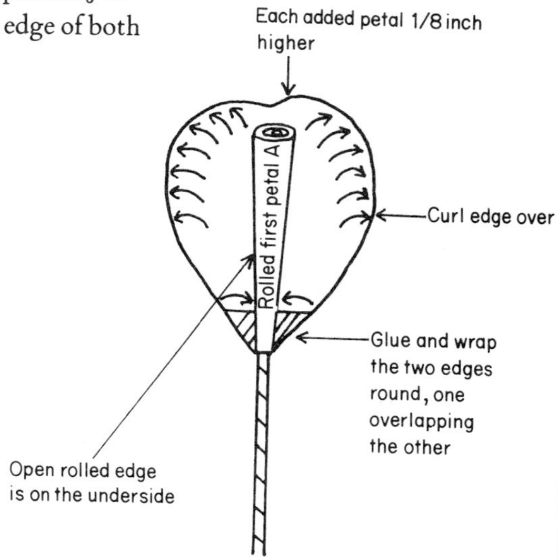

Fig 9.3

Measure $\frac{3}{4}$ in from the top of the last attached petal A. Cut several $\frac{1}{2}$ in wide strips of paper tissue and commence to wind them round, starting at the $\frac{3}{4}$ in mark. Add plenty of glue as you wind and also twist the tissue strip at every turn, thus building up a good rounded bud shape. Continue to pad until the bud is about 2 in in circumference. A larger amount of padding may be added if a bigger and fatter bud is required. When the padding is completed, cut a $\frac{1}{2}$ in wide strip of crepe in the same colour as the rose being made. Cover the padded area with glue and stick the strip round, covering the entire bud. *See Fig 9.4.*

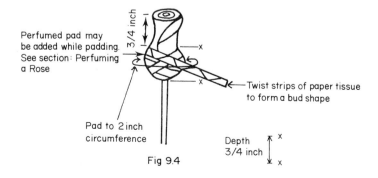

Perfumed pad may be added while padding. See section: Perfuming a Rose

3/4 inch

Pad to 2 inch circumference

Twist strips of paper tissue to form a bud shape

Depth 3/4 inch

Fig 9.4

Three size A petals remain, curl each one at the top as before and shape them into a bowl at the base, also curl them inwards at the bottom as shown in *Fig 9.5*. The petals now look exactly like real rose petals. This shaping especially at the base is what gives a realistic result.

Paint a little glue on the hatched area of the first one and place it so that the open-rolled edge on the prepared bud lies face down onto the centre of the petal. Make sure the petal being added is ⅛ in higher, as previously explained. The glued area is then stuck down onto the padded area of the bud. A small spot of glue should be added on either side of the petal base to hold it in place. *See Fig 9.6*.

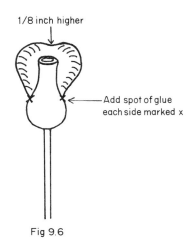

1/8 inch higher

Add spot of glue each side marked x

Fig 9.6

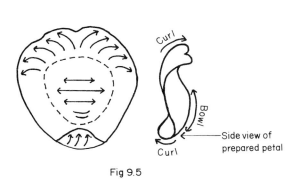

Curl

Bowl

Curl

Side view of prepared petal

Fig 9.5

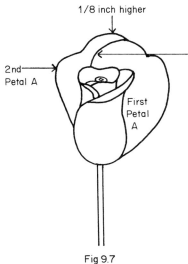

1/8 inch higher

2nd Petal A

First Petal A

Left hand edge of last petal on the bud is placed at the halfway mark of the next petal to be affixed

Fig 9.7

The second petal A, having been curled and bowled, is attached again ⅛ in higher. The left hand edge of the last petal on the bud is placed at the halfway mark of the one now being affixed. Likewise, the third petal A is glued ⅛ in higher, and the left hand edge of the previous one lined up with the centre of the third petal A. *See Fig 9.7*.

Take the first petal B, curl and bowl as for A. Glue the hatched area and affix with the left-hand edge of the last petal A not to the halfway mark as before but about one third of the way instead. As the rose increases in size, the petals have to be spread slightly further apart, otherwise the flower would be too tight, and the petals unable to open out. Continue in the way described, working round the rose, not forgetting each petal is $\frac{1}{8}$ in higher than the previous one. (When all petals B have been attached you will have a nice rose bud and you may wish to stop and not add any more petals. Long-stemmed buds are very attractive; directions for completion are the same as for the full-size rose.)

Full-size rose

Bowl and curl the C petals of which there are four. Continue working round as before, spreading each petal a little further apart as explained above.

Having curled and bowled the four D petals, glue the hatched area and arrange the four evenly spaced round the flower. They will be slightly overlapping at the edges. Always try to place the petals between the joins of ones already attached, never have two petals one directly behind the other. Also, do not forget still to place each new petal $\frac{1}{8}$ in higher than the one before. Finally, bowl and curl the E petals of which there are five. Make a small pleat at the bottom of each petal before spreading the glue on the hatched area. The five petals are arranged round the flower and attached. To shape the flower, place the tips of the fingers of both hands on the inside of the petal base and with thumbs on the outside, gently re-shape the bowled petals and generally open them out. Work round each layer in turn, some of the tips of the petals may also be frilled a little by stretching the top edge between fingers and thumbs.

A little padding should now be added to prepare the area beneath the flower head for the calyx petals. Cut $\frac{1}{2}$ in wide paper tissue strips, and wind and twist them round using ample glue. The size of the padded area should be $1\frac{3}{4}$ in in circumference $\times \frac{1}{2}$ in deep. *See Fig 9.8.*

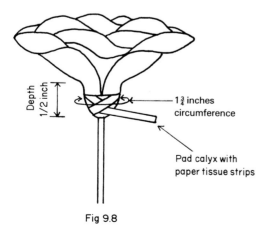

Fig 9.8

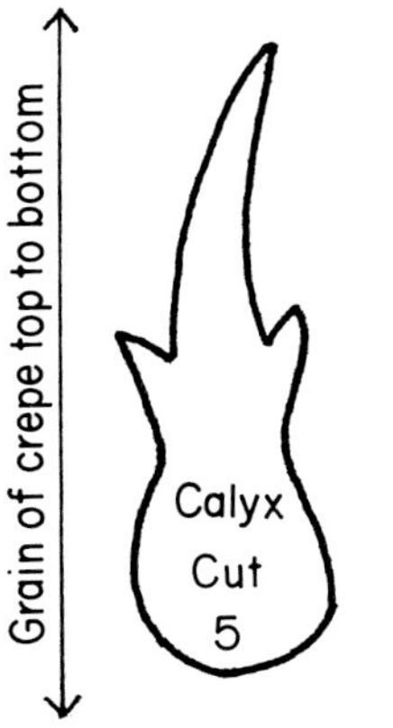
Grain of crepe top to bottom
Calyx
Cut
5

Fig 9.9 Pattern

The calyx petals are cut from leaf-green double crepe paper. Prepare a section in advance and leave to dry before cutting the five calyx petals. The grain of crepe should be top to bottom when cutting out calyx petals.

Cut a strip of leaf-green crepe paper $\frac{1}{2}$ in wide. Commencing underneath the flower head, cover the padded area. Use plenty of glue and gather the strip in so that it fits round smoothly. Continue down the stem leaving the bottom 1 in uncovered. Re-wind from the bottom up the stem, terminating at the base of the calyx padding. Colour the calyx petals as shown *Fig 9.10*. The coloured area is bent over and the tip curled with the edge of the ruler. *See Fig 9.11*. Paint glue on the dotted area of the first calyx petal and place glued section onto prepared padded area beneath the flower head. *See Fig 9.11*.

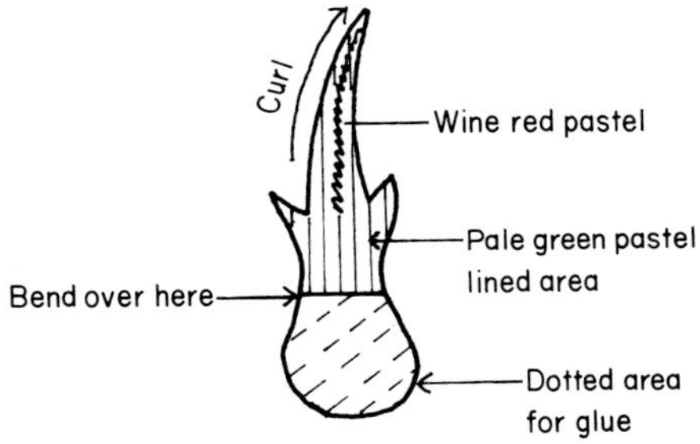
Curl
Wine red pastel
Pale green pastel
lined area
Bend over here
Dotted area
for glue

Fig 9.10

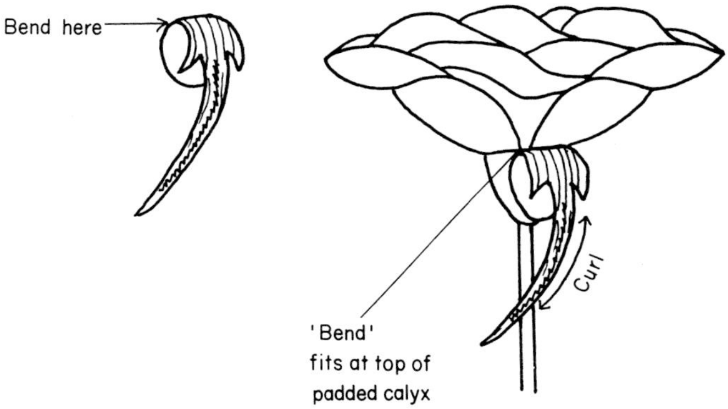
Bend here
Curl
'Bend'
fits at top of
padded calyx

Fig 9.11

The remaining four calyx petals are evenly spaced round the padded area in the same way. Each one is curled as shown, with the pale green and red coloured area on the outside. The stem of the rose is now coloured using the wine-red pastel crayon. Leave small spaces where the thorns are to be attached uncoloured as the glue will not hold on top of the pastel. Smooth the stem after the colour has been applied to blend it. If the rose leaf sprays are to be attached to the flower stem, it is best to put the thorns on afterwards, otherwise they are in the way when binding on the leaves. Rose thorns may be gathered from the rose bush in the garden; they are glued onto the stem. (Look at the real stem to see the spacing.) Usually the first thorn is approximately 3 in from the base of the flower. The smaller thorns are at the top and the larger ones at the bottom. Paint each one with clear nail varnish to preserve.

PERFUMING A ROSE

A paper rose which is perfumed is an added novelty! There are several rose-scented perfumes available from large chemists or stores.

A small piece of cotton-wool soaked in the perfume and allowed to dry is all that is required. The scented cotton-wool is then wrapped round when padding the rose bud *(Fig 9.4)*. Just add the cotton-wool in place of several of the paper-tissue strips. Glue the crepe-paper strip to cover the cotton-wool as described.

Another way of perfuming the completed rose is to place the flower in a polythene bag together with the perfumed pad of cotton-wool. Secure the neck of the bag firmly by tying round the stem and leave for about a week. The crepe paper absorbs the perfume and it will be quite lasting.

A single long-stemmed perfumed rose makes a very nice gift, and is very inexpensive!

ROSE LEAVES

Materials

Plain newspaper, obtainable from a newspaper printing office. If not available a cheap quality child's plain drawing pad will do
Rose wires
Sap green Winsor & Newton acrylic paint No 348
Fairly stiff paint brush – hog bristle ($\frac{1}{4}$ in width)
Jam jar lid
Leaf-green crepe paper
Pale green, dark-wine red, dark-brown pastel crayons
12-inch ruler. Lead pencil (B)
Tracing paper. Sharp scissors
Adhesive (Latex-type)
Thin card for templates
Thick yellow felt-tip pen, (the tip should be $\frac{1}{4}$ in wide)
Orange felt-tip pen
Wooden cocktail stick (for marking veins)

It is advisable to prepare two leaf sprays at one time, thus when painting, the first spray can be put aside to dry while the second spray is painted.

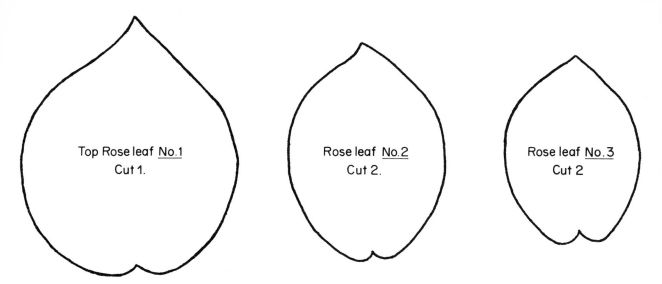

Fig. 9.12 Leaf Patterns

Within the figure:
Top Rose leaf No.1
Cut 1.

Rose leaf No.2
Cut 2.

Rose leaf No.3
Cut 2

One-leaf spray

Cover three rose wires with a $\frac{1}{4}$ in wide strip of leaf-green crepe paper. The rose-leaf patterns are given in *Fig 9.12*. Lay the templates on the plain newspaper and draw round each one with a pencil, then cut out the five leaves.

Glue one rose wire down the centre of leaf No 1. Glue the second wire down centre of one of the leaves No 2. Glue the other No 2 leaf to the other end of the same wire, e.g. one leaf at each end. Likewise, using the third wire, glue a No 3 leaf at each end. *See Fig 9.13*.

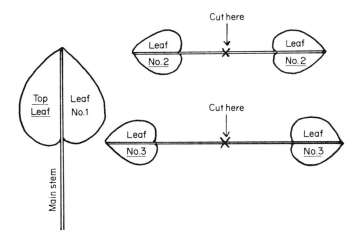

Fig. 9.13 Showing how to glue the 3 rose wires to the 5 leaves

The wire with a leaf No 2 on either end is then cut in the centre area marked with a 'x' in *Fig 9.13*. Likewise, the remaining two No 3 leaves are cut to separate in the same way.

The two No 2 leaves are then glued on either side of the main stem which already has leaf No 1 affixed to the top. Bind both leaves with a ¼ in wide strip of leaf-green crepe when they are both glued in place on the main stem. The last two No 3 leaves are then affixed underneath in the same way and bound as before. *See Fig 9.14*.

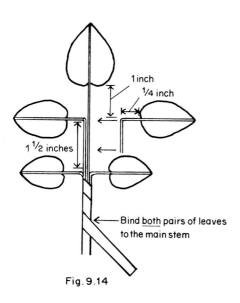

Fig. 9.14

The edges of all the leaves are then snipped using sharp scissors. *See Fig 9.15*. The leaves are now prepared for painting. Mix a small amount of sap green paint on the lid of a jam jar. Use enough water to thin the paint, but not so much as to soak through the thin newspaper. It is a good idea to practise on a spare piece of paper to get it just right. All painting strokes and strokes using the felt pen should follow the shape of the leaf. Work from the centre vein outwards, not straight up and down. Paint the backs of all five leaves pale green.

When they are dry, paint the topside of the leaves, using the paint much thicker. While the paint is still wet, rub the blade of the scissors along the centre vein of each leaf, thus scraping a little of the paint off and exposing the centre vein. Care should be taken to do this gently and not tear the wet paper.

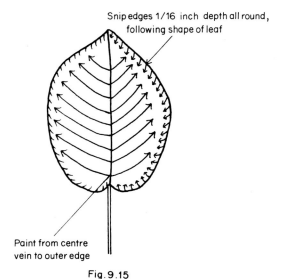

Snip edges 1/16 inch depth all round, following shape of leaf

Paint from centre vein to outer edge

Fig. 9.15

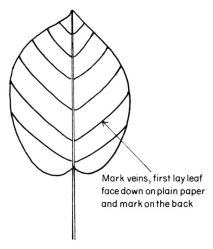

Mark veins, first lay leaf face down on plain paper and mark on the back

Fig. 9.16

When the painted leaves are quite dry, paint over the topside of each one (one at a time) using a broad-tipped yellow felt pen. While the leaf is still damp, turn it over face down onto a piece of plain white paper. Proceed to mark the veins on the back of the leaf, as shown in *Fig 9.16* using a cocktail stick.

The leaf should then be gently peeled off the paper on which it has been laid. Some of the colour will have come off in patches where it has been pressed down onto the paper while damp. A little orange felt-tip lightly 'brushed' over some of these areas makes the leaf have a brown tinge, this gives a realistic effect and enhances the natural appearance.

Stipule pattern

Snip edges both sides

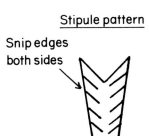

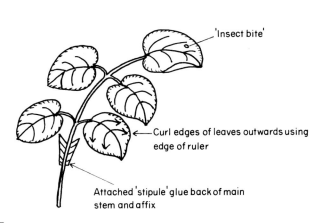

'Insect bite'

Curl edges of leaves outwards using edge of ruler

Attached 'stipule' glue back of main stem and affix

Fig. 9.17

The remaining four leaves of the spray are all painted in turn, and the veins marked as described. Having completed this operation, colour all the stems of the leaves and the main stem using a dark red pastel crayon. Brush a very light stroke of pale green pastel up the centre vein of each leaf. Small holes and blemishes in the leaves can be made as follows: push the point of the cocktail stick through the leaf and make a small hole. Using the point of a dark brown pastel, insert it into the hole and twist the crayon once. This gives a very realistic insect bite mark.

The leaf edges are then curled with the edge of a ruler, and bent into shape as shown in *Fig 9.17*. Cut a stipule from single leaf-green crepe, pattern *Fig 9.17*. Colour both sides lightly with a dark red pastel. Paint a little glue on the underside of the main leaf stem and affix the stipule. *See Fig 9.17*. The completed leaf is then glued to the main stem of the rose, and bound with a leaf-green strip of crepe to secure. Glue real rose thorns to the stem and paint them with clear nail varnish. To complete, colour the remainder of the rose stem with the red pastel. *See Fig 9.18* for the completed rose.

Fig. 9.18 Complete Rose

10. African Daisy

A bright daisy-like flower, very dainty, on a long, slim stem.

Materials

Duplex crepe in pink with purple
Single crepe paper in very pale yellow, deep yellow and pale green
Green plastic-covered wire for stem, 2 mm thick
Pastel crayons in black, pale yellow, dark wine-red and white
Adhesive (Latex-type)
Small, very sharp scissors
12-inch ruler
Thin card for templates
Tracing paper
Lead pencil (B)
Pliers
Fine point black felt-tip pen

White daisy   Materials are the same as above except for the addition of duplex white crepe.

AFRICAN DAISY FLOWER AND LEAVES

Cut a length of 2 mm thickness stem wire 13 in long, and cover the top
$2\frac{1}{2}$ in with a $\frac{1}{4}$ in wide strip of pale yellow crepe paper. Wind round and
secure with spots of glue. Bend the top over and form a $\frac{1}{4}$ in hook. Close
the hook using the pliers. Cut a section of pale yellow crepe paper (grain
running from top to bottom) size $\frac{1}{2}$ in deep × 4 in long. *See Fig 10.1.*

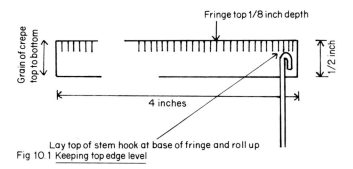

Fig 10.1 Keeping top edge level

Fold this piece of crepe in half, then in quarters. Fringe the top edge finely
all the way along to a depth of $\frac{1}{8}$ in. Open out, and taking the stem, cover
the hook with glue and place the top of the hook at the base of the fringe.
See Fig 10.1. Proceed to wind round and round, keeping the top level and
adding spots of glue at regular intervals. Cut a second piece of crepe
paper, deep yellow this time, size the same as for the first. Fringe the top
to a depth of $\frac{1}{8}$ in as before. Wind round on top of the first piece, keeping
the top level, adding frequent spots of glue to hold. The centre of the
flower is thus completed in pale yellow with a deeper yellow surround.
Dab a few small black spots on the pale yellow area using a fine-tipped
black felt pen.

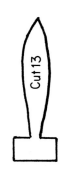

Fig 10.2 Petal Pattern

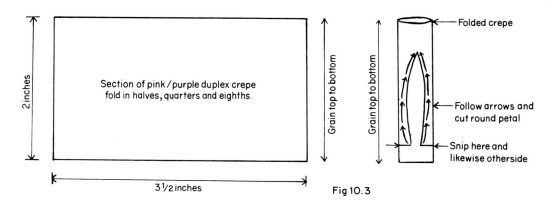

Fig 10.3

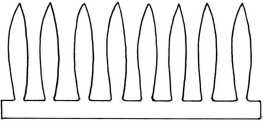

Fig 10.4 <u>Eight petals in a row all joined</u>

Cut a section of duplex pink/purple crepe, size 2 in deep × 3½ in long (grain running top to bottom). Fold this piece into halves, quarters, and eighths. Take the petal pattern as given in *Fig 10.2* lay the pattern on the folded paper and cut out as shown in *Fig 10.3*. You should now have eight petals in a row, all joined at the base as shown in *Fig 10.4*.

There remain five more petals to be cut out. A piece of pink/purple duplex crepe size 2 in deep × 2¼ in long is used for these. As it is composed of an odd number of petals, the crepe cannot be folded as before, therefore lay the petal template on the crepe to measure the width and then fold the crepe paper over five times. Cut out as before. Having cut out 13 petals, use a black and pale yellow pastel to colour the purple side of each petal as follows: first a light shading of pale yellow then a little black on top. *See Fig 10.5*.

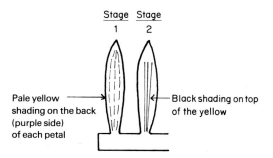

Fig 10.5 <u>Colouring of petals (Purple side)</u>

The pink side of each petal has white pastel shading with a little dark-wine red either side at the base of each one. *See Fig 10.6*. When all 13 petals have been coloured as described, curl the tip of each one using the edge of a ruler.

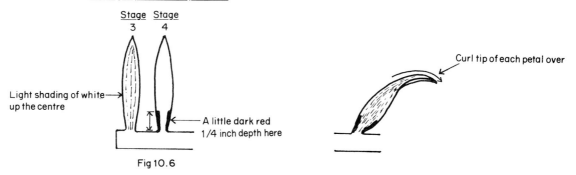

Colouring of petals (Pale pink side)

Stage Stage
3   4

Light shading of white→
up the centre

A little dark red
1/4 inch depth here

Curl tip of each petal over

Fig 10.6

The petals are now ready for attaching to the prepared centre on the stem. *See Fig 10.7.*

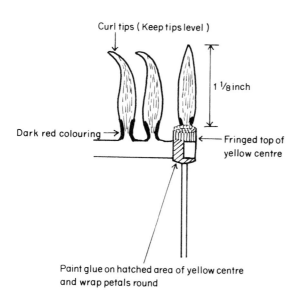

Curl tips (Keep tips level)

1 1/8 inch

Dark red colouring →

Fringed top of
yellow centre

Paint glue on hatched area of yellow centre
and wrap petals round

Fig 10.7

The tips of the petals should be $1\frac{1}{8}$ in above the top of the centre as shown in *Fig 10.7.* The pale pink side of the crepe goes on the inside. Paint glue on the hatched area of the centre, just below the fringed top, also shown in *Fig 10.7.* Proceed to wind the first strip of eight petals round and round the centre, keeping the tips level. Paint more glue on the centre as you go. Wind firmly, but do not stretch the crepe. If the petals are opened out, you will be able to see clearly when and where to spread them out. The second strip of five petals is then wound round on top of the first. Commence with the first petal lined up in a space; try not to stick two petals directly one behind the other. When all the petals have been affixed, it is easy to pull them into place arranging them in the gaps. Cut a $\frac{1}{4}$ in wide strip of pale green crepe and, starting about 1 in up from the bottom of the stem, wind firmly round it adding frequent spots of glue. When the top of the stem is reached, paint a little glue round the base of the flower to a depth of about $\frac{1}{8}$ in. Continue winding the stem strip to cover the base of the flower. Gather in and squeeze under the flower head thus giving a neat finish. *See Fig 10.8.*

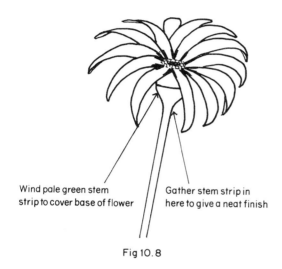

Wind pale green stem strip to cover base of flower

Gather stem strip in here to give a neat finish

Fig 10.8

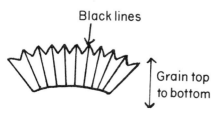

Black lines

Grain top to bottom

Fig 10.9 Calyx Pattern

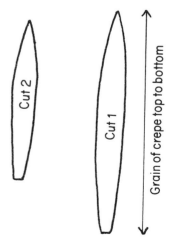

Cut 2

Cut 1

Grain of crepe top to bottom

Fig 10.10 Leaf Patterns

Prepare a section of pale green double crepe by glueing two pieces together; the calyx and leaves are cut from this. An easy way to cut the tiny 'v' shapes at the top of the calyx is to cut round the outside line, e.g. draw an imaginary line straight along the top edge. The calyx may then be folded in half and the tiny 'v' shapes cut. Mark the black lines, as shown on the pattern in *Fig 10.9* using a sharp-pointed black-lead pencil. Stretch the calyx by pulling from each side gently. Apply a little glue round the inside bottom and side edges only, the black lines going on the outside. Wrap the calyx round the base of the flower as shown in *Fig 10.11*. Cut the leaves, two small and one large. Mark a centre vein on each by pressing along the leaf with a pointed wooden cocktail stick. Colour either side of the vein lightly with the black pastel crayon. (One side only – this is the inside of the leaf). Curl the tips over, and paint a small spot of glue at the base of each leaf. Attach the first small leaf $5\frac{1}{2}$ in down from the base of the calyx, the second small leaf $1\frac{1}{2}$ in lower on the opposite side of the stem. The third leaf is affixed $1\frac{1}{2}$ in lower still. *See Fig 10.11* which also shows how to bend the stem of the now completed flower.

An attractive variation of the african daisy is made in white duplex crepe paper. There are the following alterations to be made. The centre of the flower is formed using a piece of deep yellow crepe only, size $\frac{1}{2}$ in deep × 8 in long, fringed at the top edge to a depth of $\frac{1}{8}$ in as before. A few black spots are added to the completed centre as previously explained. When colouring the petals, use yellow and black on the underside in the same way as before. There is no colouring on the topside. Otherwise the instructions are the same as for the pink flower.

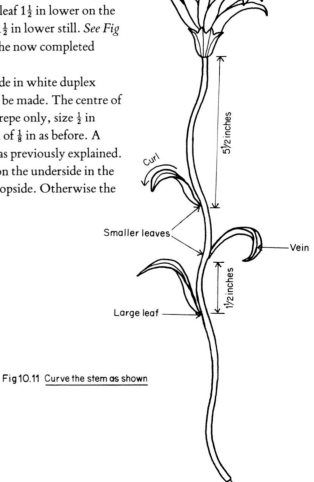

Curl

5½ inches

Smaller leaves

Vein

½ inches

Large leaf

Fig 10.11 Curve the stem as shown

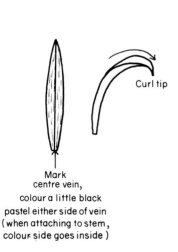

Curl tip

Mark
centre vein,
colour a little black
pastel either side of vein
(when attaching to stem,
colour side goes inside)

11. Sweet Pea

Sweet peas are available in a variety of lovely pinks and mauves. They are delicate-looking flowers which make excellent displays.

Materials

Best quality (acid free) tissue paper in a variety of pastel shades
Leaf-green crepe paper
Rose wires (obtained from a florist)
Sheet of thin card for templates
Tracing paper
Lead pencil (B)
Small, sharp scissors
Adhesive(Latex-type)
12-inch ruler
White pastel crayon
Green plastic-covered wire $1\frac{1}{4}$ mm thick for stiffening the base of the stem of a completed flower

SWEET PEA FLOWER

Select the colour of tissue paper to be used; cut the centre pod pattern given in *Fig 11.1*. When cutting, fold a small section of tissue paper in half, lay the pod pattern on this and cut round the outer edge (thus producing two pods).

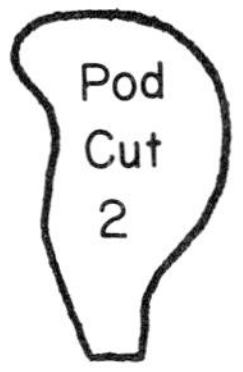

Pod
Cut
2

Fig 11.1 <u>Pattern</u>

Take one rose wire, lay one half of the pod on a flat surface and proceed to bend the top of the wire to the outer edge shape of the pod. *See Fig 11.2.* When the wire is the correct shape, e.g. like a question mark, cover the bent portion with glue and lay it down onto the pod, picking it up on one side of the glued wire. Turn the wire over and lay it down onto the second half of the pod and pick it up in the same way.

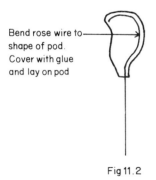

Bend rose wire to shape of pod. Cover with glue and lay on pod

Fig 11.2

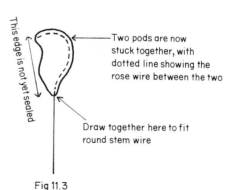

This edge is not yet sealed

Two pods are now stuck together, with dotted line showing the rose wire between the two

Draw together here to fit round stem wire

Fig 11.3

The unsealed edge as shown in *Fig 11.3* is then opened out by inserting the point of the scissors, and a small piece of crumpled tissue paper, the same colour as the pod, is pushed inside padding it out a little. The two edges are now sealed with a small amount of glue *See Figs 11.4 and 11.5*

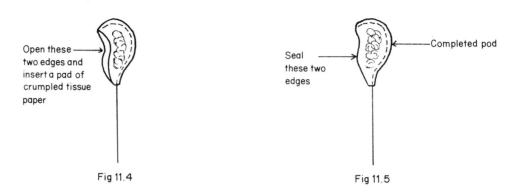

Open these two edges and insert a pad of crumpled tissue paper

Fig 11.4

Seal these two edges

Completed pod

Fig 11.5

Colour the shaded area on both sides of the pod with a white pastel crayon. *See Fig 11.6*. Cut a $\frac{1}{4}$ in wide strip of leaf-green crepe and, commencing at the base of the pod, wind round the wire, adding spots of glue until the whole stem is covered. Take the completed pod and bend as shown also in *Fig 11.6*.

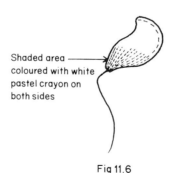

Shaded area coloured with white pastel crayon on both sides

Fig 11.6

Take a folded piece of tissue paper, lay pattern of petal A *Fig 11.7* along the folded edge as shown in *Fig 11.8*.

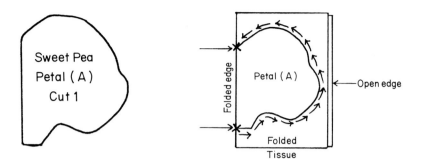

Fig 11.7 Pattern

Fig 11.8 Cut from x to x following arrows

Cut from 'x' to 'x' following the arrows. The petal A is then opened out as shown in *Fig 11.9*.

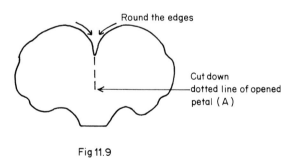

Fig 11.9

Cut down the dotted line, *see Fig 11.9*, making sure the top edges are nicely rounded. Using a white pastel crayon, shade petal A outside and inside, as shown in *Fig 11.10 & 11.11*.

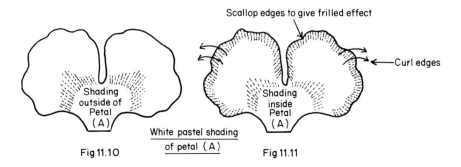

Fig 11.10

White pastel shading of petal (A)

Fig 11.11

94

When the shading has been completed, gently rub with the finger tip to smooth the pastel and erase hard lines. The whole effect should be soft. Small pieces are cut out round the outer edge of the petal to give a slightly frilled effect. *See Fig 11.11*. Curl the edge over from the inside also shown in *Fig 11.11*. The petal A is now ready to be affixed to the pod.

Spread a small amount of glue along the bottom edge and wrap the petal round the base of the pod. *See Fig 11.12*.

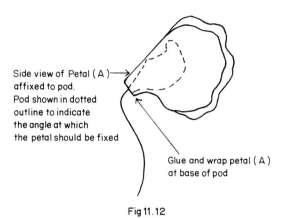

Side view of Petal (A)→
affixed to pod.
Pod shown in dotted
outline to indicate
the angle at which
the petal should be fixed

Glue and wrap petal (A)
at base of pod

Fig 11.12

Cut one size B petal, *see Fig 11.13* for pattern. Shade with white pastel the same as for petal A. Scallop the edge to give a frilled effect as before and curl outwards with the edge of the ruler.

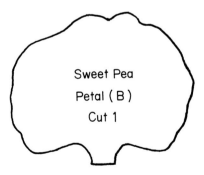

Sweet Pea

Petal (B)

Cut 1

Fig 11.13 Pattern

To affix petal B fold it loosely in half, this helps to get the petal central. Spread a little glue on the bottom tab and wrap it round at the base of the pod as before, placing it on top of petal A. *See Fig 11.14*.

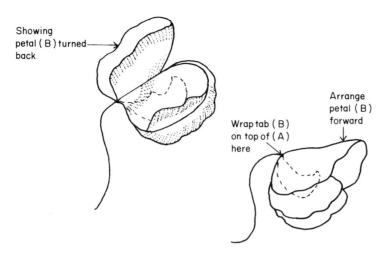

Showing petal (B) turned back

Arrange petal (B) forward

Wrap tab (B) on top of (A) here

Fig 11.14

Petal B can be arranged forward if the flower is just opening, or back if the flower is fully out. *See Fig 11.14*.

Cut a calyx from single leaf-green crepe from the pattern given in *Fig 11.15*. Curl the top edge of the calyx, and with the curled edge away from the flower, spread a little glue along the bottom edge of the calyx and wrap it round the base of the petals. Gather the base of the calyx so as it fits neatly round the stem.

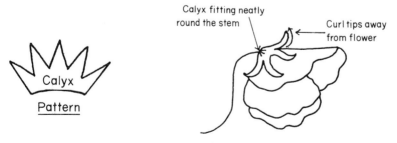

Calyx fitting neatly round the stem

Curl tips away from flower

Calyx

Pattern

Fig 11.15

Continue making four or five flowers, all of the same colour, and assemble them all on one stem. *See Fig 11.16*.

Flower No 1 is a full-length stem.

Flower No 2 is a half-length glued along one side $1\frac{1}{2}$ in down.

96

Flower No 3 is glued a further 1 in down on the opposite side, leaving the stem wire full length.

Flower No 4 is glued on the other side, again 1 in down as before, also leaving the stem uncut. Always aim to have only two stem wires at one time. If there is a third stem wire or part of a wire, trim if off. Any number of flowers may be added in this way. Bind the area where the stems have been joined on. Use a $\frac{1}{4}$ in wide strip of leaf-green crepe to do this. An extra piece of $1\frac{1}{4}$-mm wire may be bound at the base of the completed stem to stiffen it if required.

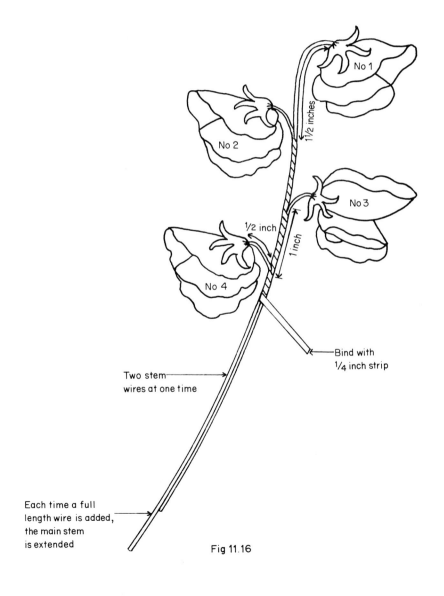

No 1

No 2

No 3

No 4

1/2 inches

1/2 inch

1 inch

Bind with
1/4 inch strip

Two stem wires at one time

Each time a full length wire is added, the main stem is extended

Fig 11.16

12. Rhododendron

This rhododendron is a very simple flower to make, it was designed with the beginner in the art of Paper Flower Sculpture in mind. The clusters of bell-shaped flowers in rich red crepe paper are wired to real rhododendron leaves making a spectacular display.

Materials

Single crepe paper in rich red and leaf green
Rose wires (obtained from a florist)
Adhesive (Latex-type)
12-inch ruler
Lead pencil (B)
Tracing paper
Thin card for pattern template
2 pairs of sharp scissors – one large and one small
Yellow poster colour (Winsor & Newton)
Small paint brush
Pliers

RHODODENDRON FLOWER

Take three rose wires, cut long strips of red crepe paper $\frac{1}{4}$ in wide. (Cut across a whole fold of crepe to do this).

Paint a spot of glue on the end of the crepe strip and using a twirling action wind the paper tightly round the wire, putting on spots of glue at regular intervals. See the section in Chapter 1 on winding rose wires. When the three wires are covered, cut them up into eight stamens making them varied lengths. *See Fig 12.1*. Paint a spot of glue on the ends which have been cut to make sure they do not come undone.

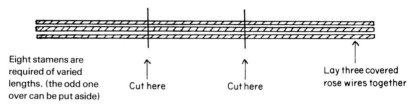

Eight stamens are required of varied lengths. (the odd one over can be put aside)

Cut here

Cut here

Lay three covered rose wires together

Fig 12.1

Cover another rose wire as before, using this as a stem with the end as a stigma. Arrange the eight stamens round it with the stigma protruding $\frac{1}{2}$ in above the tips of the stamens.

Secure at the base of the stamens with glue, bind with a $\frac{1}{4}$ in wide strip of red crepe to hold them securely. *See Fig 12.2*.

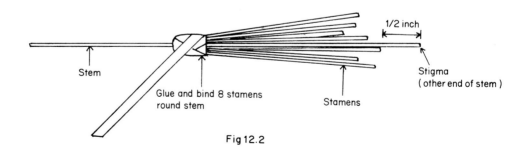

1/2 inch

Stem

Glue and bind 8 stamens round stem

Stamens

Stigma (other end of stem)

Fig 12.2

Spread the stamens out a little and paint a small spot of yellow poster colour on the tip of each one including the stigma. Put on one side to dry while the flower is made.

For the flower cut a cardboard petal from the pattern given in *Fig 12.3*.

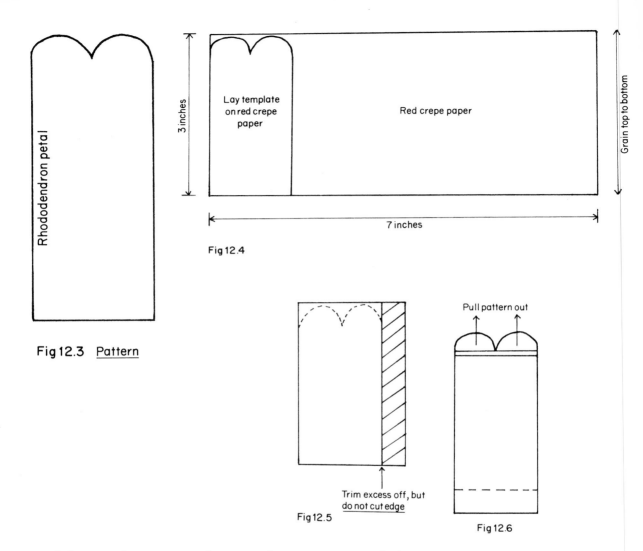

Rhododendron petal

3 inches

Lay template on red crepe paper

Red crepe paper

Grain top to bottom

7 inches

Fig 12.4

Fig 12.3   Pattern

Trim excess off, but do not cut edge

Fig 12.5

Pull pattern out

Fig 12.6

With the grain of paper running from top to bottom, cut a piece of red crepe 3 in deep × 7 in long. Lay the petal pattern on one end of this and proceed to fold the crepe over four times with the pattern template inside. Leaving the crepe folded, gently ease the pattern out from the centre by pulling with your finger-tips from the top. See *Figs 12.4, 12.5, 12.6,* and *12.7* which show the stage by stage cutting out of a flower.

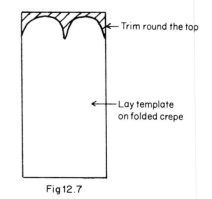

Trim round the top

Lay template on folded crepe

Fig 12.7

Having removed the pattern from the centre of the folded crepe, *(Fig 12.6)* and trimmed any excess paper from the side *(Fig 12.5)*, lay the petal template on the folded crepe and cut round the top *(Fig 12.7)*.

When the top has been cut out, unfold the crepe and the result is shown in *Fig 12.8*.

100

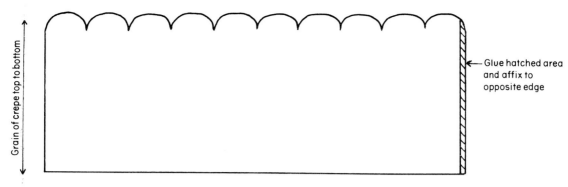

Fig 12.8

Spread a very small strip of glue along the hatched edge, as shown in *Fig 12.8*, and join to the opposite edge, forming a bell shape. Take the bell shape (or flower) and paint glue round the inside bottom edge to a depth of about $\frac{1}{8}$ in. The stem with the stamens at the top is then threaded down through the centre of the flower from the top. Line the *base* of the stamens up with the glued edge at the bottom of the flower, the top ends of the stamens should not protrude beyond the top edge of the flower. Gather in and affix to the stem.

Snip down about $\frac{1}{8}$ in between each of the petals, stretch the top edge, and curl each petal outwards. Finally, frill the tips of the petals.

To arrange the stamens grasp the base of the flower with the left hand, and with the other hand take hold of the bunch of stamens inside the flower. Bend them down first then bend the tips upwards. *See Fig 12.9.* Separate each stamen and spread them out inside the flower.

Cut a $\frac{1}{4}$ in wide strip of leaf-green crepe and, commencing at the base of the flower, wind round and cover the stem, add spots of glue at regular intervals to secure.

Make seven more flowers as described and arrange them in a bunch. Starting about $1\frac{1}{2}$ in down the stems, bind them all together with a $\frac{1}{2}$ in wide strip of leaf-green crepe. The completed cluster is then wired to a spray of *real* rhododendron leaves. It is possible to make rhododendron leaves from thin card but, due to the large number required for a display, it is not very practicable. You may wish, however, to make one spray and the instructions which follow will enable this to be done.

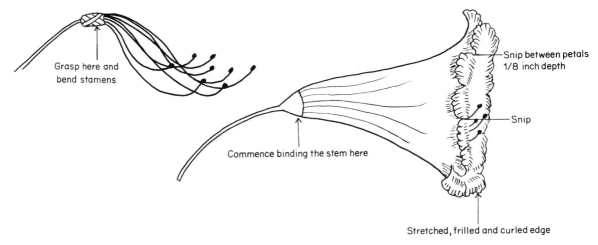

Grasp here and
bend stamens

Snip between petals
1/8 inch depth

Commence binding the stem here

Snip

Stretched, frilled and curled edge

Fig 12.9 <u>Completed Flower</u>

RHODODENDRON LEAVES

Instructions for making one spray of leaves:

Materials

A sheet of thin yellow card (available from an art shop)
Leaf-green crepe paper
Thick yellow felt-tip pen (the felt-tip should be $\frac{1}{4}$ in wide)
Artists acrylic colour sap green, No 348 (Winsor & Newton)
Fairly coarse approximately $\frac{1}{4}$ in width hogshair paint brush
12-inch length of green plastic covered wire 2 mm thick
Thirteen florists wires 7 in long × 0.9 mm thick
Paper tissues for padding the bud
Adhesive (Latex-type)
Lead pencil (B), tracing paper, thin card for templates
Large and small sharp scissors
Jam jar lid for mixing the paint on
Dark wine red pastel crayon
Pliers

Trace and cut out templates for 13 leaves, there are 12 given in *Fig 12.10*.
Cut two of the larger ones as marked. Lay the templates on the yellow
card and cut them out.

Cover 13 florists wires with $\frac{1}{4}$ in wide strips of leaf-green crepe. Wind
the strips round and secure with spots of glue. Glue a covered wire down
the centre vein of each leaf.

To paint the leaves mix some sap green acrylic paint in the jam jar lid, and using a little water mix to a thin paste. Paint the underside of all the leaves, working from the centre vein to the outer edge with the brush strokes. When dry, paint the topside with two-coats of paint to give a good, smooth matt colour. Brush strokes are as for the underside.

When the painting is completed and the leaves are thoroughly dry, lay each leaf in turn onto a pad of newspaper, topside uppermost. Coat each side of the centre vein with the thick yellow felt tip, working towards the outer edge to the shape of the leaf. When the whole surface has been covered, rub the felt pen up the centre vein. Wait for approximately two minutes for the felt tip to dry, turn the leaf over and using the scissor points mark the veins.

Having prepared all 13 leaves, take the 12 in 2 mm thickness wire and cover the top 2 in with a $\frac{1}{4}$ in wide leaf-green crepe paper strip. Make a small hook of about $\frac{1}{4}$ in in depth, glue a few strips of paper tissue round the hook to form a small bud. Wind and twist the strips to obtain the bud shape. *See Fig 12.11*. (The size of bud is $\frac{1}{2}$ in deep × $\frac{3}{4}$ in circumference). Cover the bud with a further leaf-green strip, and continue down the stem to the bottom.

Commencing from directly below the bud, attach the top seven leaves (one at a time), varying the sizes, but including the two larger leaves. Measure $\frac{1}{2}$ in from the base of the first leaf down the stem wire, bend the wire at a right angle at this point. Measure a further 1 in down the wire and cut off the remainder.

Paint glue along one side of the bottom inch and attach it to the main stem (at the base of the bud) binding the area which has been joined, using a strip of leaf-green crepe $\frac{1}{4}$ in wide × approximately 4 in long. Use ample glue, and bind firmly to prevent the attached leaf from becoming loose.

Affix *three* more leaves on one side of the main stem and *two* on the opposite side. Each one should be placed approximately $\frac{1}{4}$ in lower than the one above. All are bound to the main stem as before. The remaining leaf is affixed on the *front* of the main stem wire.

The lower six leaves have $\frac{3}{4}$ in stem wire at the base, and a further $1\frac{1}{2}$ in to glue to the main stem. Place *three* leaves on one side, each $\frac{1}{4}$ in lower than the one above. *Two* more go on the opposite side, and the remaining *one* is glued to the front of the main stem. A little wine-red pastel is applied to the base of the stem of each leaf. Bend and arrange the spray using *Fig 12.11* as a guide. The cluster of rhododendron flowers is then wired to the leaf spray.

Fig. 12.10 <u>Leaf Patterns</u>

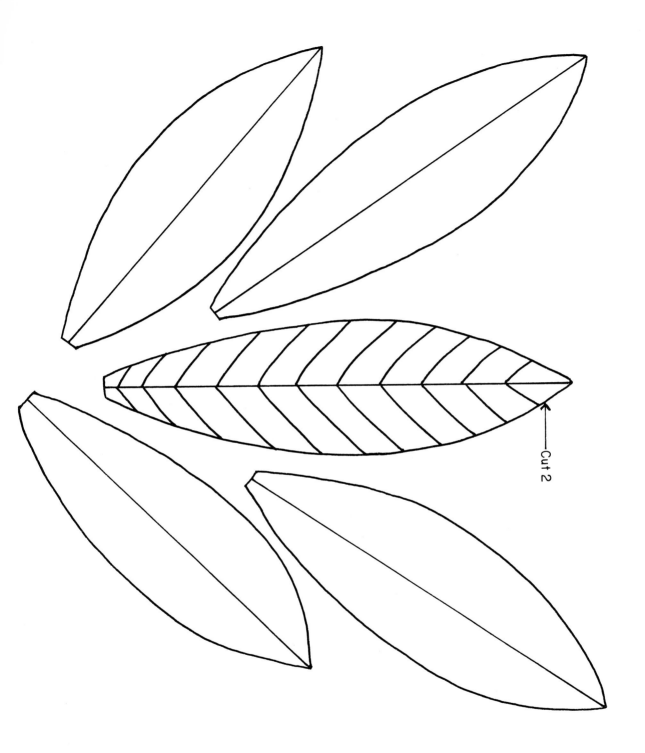

Cut 2

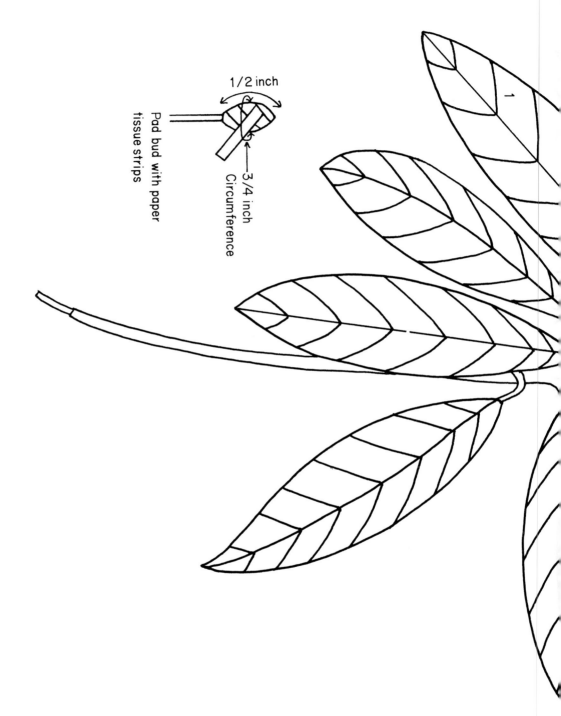

1/2 inch

Pad bud with paper
tissue strips

3/4 inch
Circumference

Fig. 12.11 Assembling a leaf spray (*This is not a pattern.*)

Attach top 7 leaves first

13. *Water Lily*

Placed on a circular mirror, the water lily is a very attractive centre piece for the dinner table. A pink flower waxes beautifully.

Materials

White duplex crepe paper (double-thickness), and two shades of yellow duplex crepe (deep yellow one side, pale the other)
Leaf-green single crepe paper
Green plastic-covered wire 2 mm thick
Paper tissues for padding
Pastel crayons in dark-wine red, pale yellow, black and yellow ochre, also pale green
Lead pencil (B)
12-inch ruler
Tracing paper
Thin card for pattern templates
2 pairs of sharp scissors – one large and one small
Adhesive(Latex-type)
Pliers

WATER LILY FLOWER

Cut a length of stem wire $3\frac{1}{2}$ in long, cover same with a $\frac{1}{4}$ in wide strip of leaf-green crepe, glued well top and bottom. Bend the wire over at the top to form a $\frac{1}{2}$ in hook. Cut some $\frac{1}{2}$ in wide paper tissues strips, and using ample glue, proceed to wind and twist them round the stem hook. The shape and dimensions are given in *Fig 13.1*. If enough glue is applied, the paper tissues become quite easy to mould into shape with your fingers. The flat top can be obtained by pressing down firmly with the thumbs. The circumference should be $3\frac{1}{4}$ in and the depth should be about $\frac{3}{4}$ in.

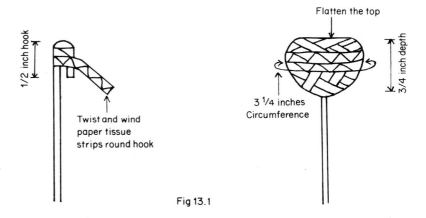

Fig 13.1

To cut the stamens for the centre of the flower, use the duplex crepe paper in two shades of yellow. Cut a length $1\frac{1}{2}$ in deep × 12 in long (grain of paper running top to bottom). *See Fig 13.2*. Divide the 12 in length into four sections, each one 3 in wide × $1\frac{1}{2}$ in depth.

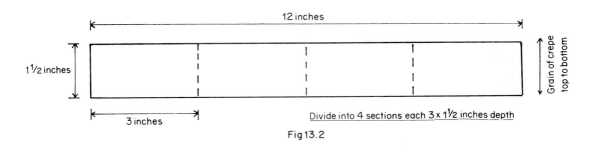

Fig 13.2

Take the first 3 in × 1½ in section and fold in half, then in quarters and finally in eighths. Lay the pattern template A as given in *Fig 13.3*, onto this and cut out eight stamens as shown in *Fig 13.4*.

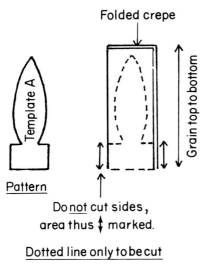

Folded crepe

Template A

Grain top to bottom

Pattern

Do <u>not</u> cut sides, area thus ↕ marked.

<u>Dotted line only to be cut</u>

Fig 13.3

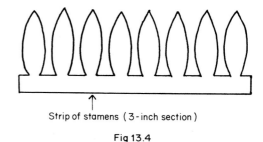

Strip of stamens (3 - inch section)

Fig 13.4

The remaining three sections are folded and cut using template A and the same method. Colour each section as shown in *Fig 13.5*.

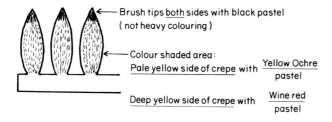

── Brush tips <u>both</u> sides with black pastel (not heavy colouring)

── Colour shaded area:
Pale yellow side of crepe with <u>Yellow Ochre</u> pastel

Deep yellow side of crepe with <u>Wine red</u> pastel

Fig 13.5 <u>Colouring for template (A)</u>

Cut a further strip of yellow duplex crepe paper, size 1½ in depth × 12 in length, (grain running from top to bottom as before). Cut into two pieces, each 1½ in deep × 6 in wide. Fold each 6 in section in turn into halves, quarters then eighths. Lay template B, see *Fig 13.6* for pattern, onto the folded crepe and cut out the same as for template A. Please note that the pastel colouring is wine red with black tips *both* sides of template B. *See Fig 13.7*.

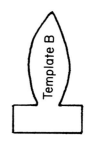

Template B

Fig 13.6 <u>Pattern</u>

110

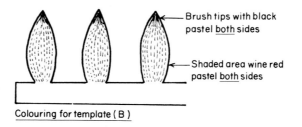

Brush tips with black pastel <u>both</u> sides

Shaded area wine red pastel <u>both</u> sides

Colouring for template (B)

Fig 13.7

Pick up the stem with the 'shape' on top, and cover the whole of the top and the sides with glue. Take first section, template A, and with the pale yellow side on the inside, wind it round the shape and press to the top edge as shown in *Fig 13.8*. The tips of the stamens should meet into a point and the padded top of the shape should not be visible.

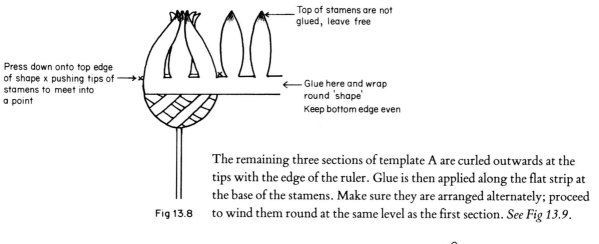

Top of stamens are not glued, leave free

Press down onto top edge of shape x pushing tips of stamens to meet into a point

Glue here and wrap round 'shape' Keep bottom edge even

Fig 13.8

The remaining three sections of template A are curled outwards at the tips with the edge of the ruler. Glue is then applied along the flat strip at the base of the stamens. Make sure they are arranged alternately; proceed to wind them round at the same level as the first section. *See Fig 13.9.*

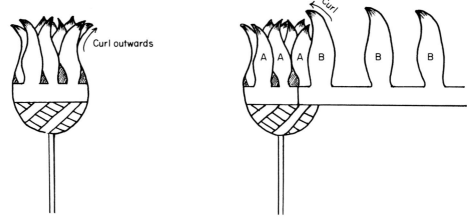

Curl outwards

Fig 13.9 Affixing template (A)

Curl

A A A B   B   B

Fig 13.10 Affixing template (B)

111

The tips of the two sections of template B are curled *inwards* and glued round at the same level, making sure the stamens are alternately spaced as before. See *Fig 13.10*. The centre of the water lily is now complete. Cut the petals from white duplex crepe paper, (with the grain of crepe running from top to bottom). Pattern templates are given in *Fig 13.13*.

Colour, bowl and curl petals numbers 1 to 4, as shown in *Fig 13.11*.

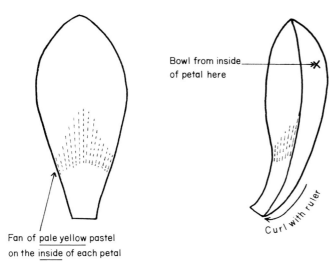

Bowl from inside of petal here

Curl with ruler

Fan of pale yellow pastel on the inside of each petal

Fig 13.11

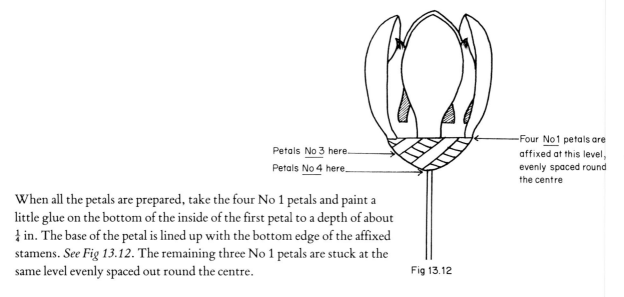

Petals No 3 here
Petals No 4 here

Four No 1 petals are affixed at this level, evenly spaced round the centre

When all the petals are prepared, take the four No 1 petals and paint a little glue on the bottom of the inside of the first petal to a depth of about $\frac{1}{4}$ in. The base of the petal is lined up with the bottom edge of the affixed stamens. *See Fig 13.12*. The remaining three No 1 petals are stuck at the same level evenly spaced out round the centre.

Fig 13.12

112

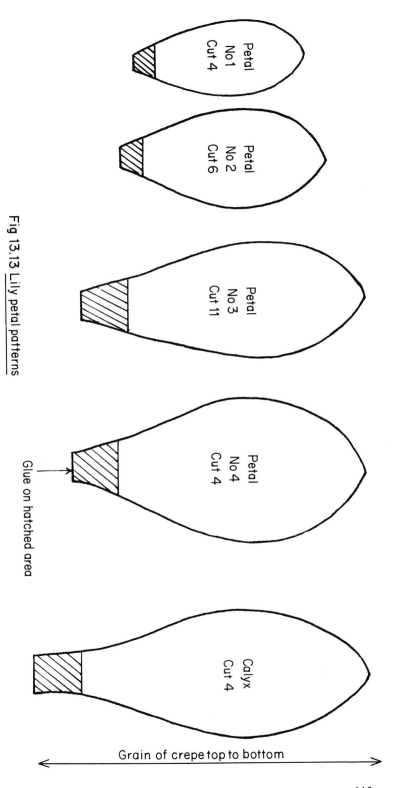

Petal
No 1
Cut 4

Petal
No 2
Cut 6

Petal
No 3
Cut 11

Petal
No 4
Cut 4

Glue on hatched area

Calyx
Cut 4

Fig 13.13 Lily petal patterns

Grain of crepe top to bottom

113

No 2 Petals   Paint glue on the bottom inside of the petal to a depth of
$\frac{1}{4}$ in as before. Affix at the same level as for No 1. As there are six petals,
place four in the spaces between the No 1 petals; the remaining two can
be placed at random.

No 3 Petals   These are attached approximately $\frac{1}{4}$ in lower than Nos 1 &
2. Paint glue to a depth of $\frac{1}{2}$ in on the bottom inside edge of petals and
arrange them round the centre, taking care always to place each one in a
space between two others already attached. Open the flower out as you
work to enable you to see the shape, and to assess where to place each
new petal, thus maintaining a good round lily.

Size 4 petals are also attached a further $\frac{1}{4}$ in lower, and the glue spread to a
depth of $\frac{1}{2}$ in as for size 3 petals. When these have been evenly spaced
round the flower, the whole of the underside of the padded shape should
be covered with the petals.

Lily calyx   The four calyx petals are coloured as shown in *Fig 13.14*.
Please note: the bowling of the calyx petals is slightly lower and the tips
are curled a little. Paint glue on the bottom inside edge to a depth of $\frac{1}{2}$ in,
as before, and arrange evenly spaced around the underside of the lily.

The white lily has pointed ends to the petals. To achieve this, apply a very
small spot of glue to the tip of each petal and pinch together. The
pinching together of the tips of the petals also gives them a good bowl
shape.

A pink water lily is made with white duplex crepe, and using the dark-
wine red-pastel crayon to shade both sides of the petals. The colour is first
applied, then blended using a small pad of cotton wool. This colour lily
waxes beautifully. *See Fig 13.15.*

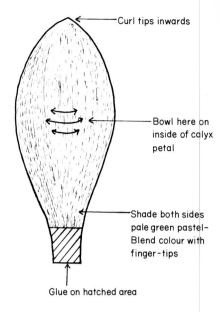

Curl tips inwards

Bowl here on
inside of calyx
petal

Shade both sides
pale green pastel-
Blend colour with
finger-tips

Glue on hatched area

Fig 13.14 Colouring of Calyx

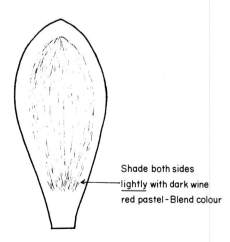

Shade both sides
lightly with dark wine
red pastel-Blend colour

Fig 13.15 Pink Water Lily Petal

114

WAXING A WATER-LILY

Materials

Half a dozen white wax candles (or paraffin wax), skewer, large saucepan, pyrex basin of approximate two pint capacity. Apron and rubber gloves. Old newspaper to cover working surface at side of cooker to avoid drips having to be cleaned off afterwards!

Wax is an inflammable substance and should be handled with care. It should never be allowed to boil! Heat as follows: put a suitable level of water in the saucepan and stand the pyrex basin in this, (check that the water is low enough so as not to bubble over into the wax, but there is enough not to boil dry!) Stand the saucepan thus prepared onto a medium heat (gas or electric). Take care with gas because of the naked flame.

Put the candles into the ovenproof glass basin and melt gently. When this has taken place, remove the strings with a skewer.

The wax should be melted until it is clear and looks like water. Check there is enough to cover the flower completely, if not add another candle. Take the water lily by the stem, having first put on the rubber gloves to protect your skin. (Splashes of hot wax burn and can be painful!)

Holding the flower upside down, plunge into the melted wax until it is completely covered. Lift out quickly and hold upside down for a second to allow the surplus wax to drip off; give it a little shake to do this. It will also partly set as this happens very quickly. Turn the flower up the right way again and cup in the palm of your hand to stop the petals sagging until it is completely set. If there are any prominent drips of wax, gently coax them off with your finger-nail. (The stem is not waxed.) Assemble the flower and the leaves afterwards.

If the flower is clogged with wax and you wish to have a second attempt, you may repeat the process and melt off the original coat.

Please note: waxed flowers should not be placed near heat such as on a sunny window sill or a radiator otherwise they will melt! Waxing other flowers is not advised as they do not look natural.

To maintain waxed flowers, dust regularly and wipe over with a damp cloth every three to six months. If the wax gets cracked, just warm in front of a fan heater; if badly damaged you can always completely re-wax them.

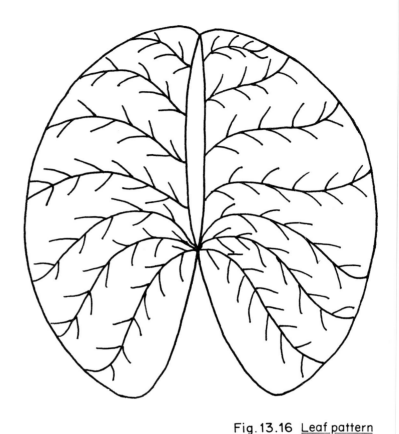

WATER LILY LEAVES

Materials

White typing paper, A4 size (71 g/m² quality)
Fine, green plastic-covered wire 1¼ mm thick
Paper tissues for padding
Artist's acrylic colour in sap green. (No 348 Winsor & Newton)
Thick yellow felt-tip pen, (¼ in wide)
Light brown felt-tip of normal thickness, e.g. ordinary felt tip
Adhesive (Latex-type)
12-inch ruler
Wooden cocktail stick for marking veins
Scissors
Pliers for bending and cutting wire
Fairly coarse approximately ¼ in width hogshair paint brush
Jam pot lid for paint mixing
Newspapers
Thin card for template
Tracing paper, Lead pencil (B)
Florist's sticky green tape
Leaf-green crepe paper

Fig.13.16 Leaf pattern

There are three leaves per flower.

Cut a leaf template from the pattern given in *Fig 13.16*.

Fold a sheet of white A4 paper into three. Lay the leaf template on this and cut out three leaves.

Also cut three sections of paper 4 in deep × $1\frac{1}{2}$ in wide from the remaining paper.

Before commencing to paint the leaves, using a pencil, mark a centre vein on one side of each leaf, as shown in *Fig 13.17*.

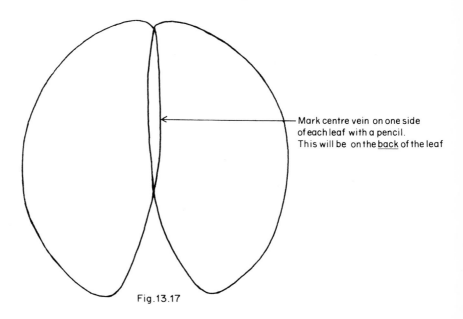

Mark centre vein on one side of each leaf with a pencil. This will be on the <u>back</u> of the leaf

Fig.13.17

When painting the leaf, the area between the two pencil lines should be left *unpainted*.

Taking the tube of sap green paint, squeeze a small amount onto the inside of the jam pot lid, moisten the brush slightly and mix the paint to a thin paste. Keep some paper tissues handy to dry off excess moisture from the brush – very little water should be used as the paper soon becomes soggy.

Proceed to spread the paint onto the back of the first leaf, taking care to leave the centre vein unpainted. Paint swiftly, and use a circular 'scrubbing' motion with the brush as shown in *Fig 13.18*. (Do one half at a time as the paint dries very quickly.) Having covered the area with paint using the circular motion, proceed with the final brush strokes, following the shape of the leaf as shown in *Fig 13.19*. While the paint is still wet, lay the painted side down onto a pad of newspaper and blot. This will dry off excess moisture and remove any brush strokes

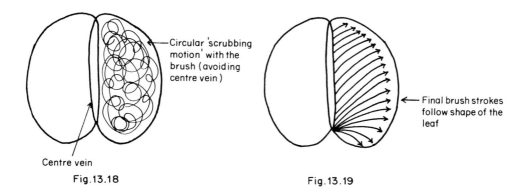

Circular 'scrubbing motion' with the brush (avoiding centre vein)

Centre vein

Fig.13.18

Final brush strokes follow shape of the leaf

Fig.13.19

giving a nice smooth finish. Complete the back of leaf in this way and set aside while you paint the backs of the remaining two.

Paint the topside as follows: apply the paint thicker on the topside, but not so thick as to give a solid look. A little variation in colour is far more natural looking. Prepare paint by mixing with a small amount of water in the lid. This time the whole leaf surface is covered. Paint one half at a time as before, using the same method, e.g. a circular scrubbing motion, followed by brushing from the centre vein outwards to the shape of the leaf, also blotting on a pad of newspaper. You will only find by experimenting the thickness of paint which gives the best effect. If, when the first layer of paint is dry, it looks too thin, repeat the process and add a second layer. The paint must be fairly thick to 'take' the yellow felt tip.

When the painted leaves are thoroughly dry, they are coated with the $\frac{1}{4}$ in wide felt pen (yellow).

The backs of the leaves are done first. Colour over the painted area on the back of each leaf in turn. Use swift strokes with the yellow felt pen, following the shape of the leaf as shown in *Fig 13.19*. When the backs of all three leaves have been completed, do the topside as follows: lay the first leaf topside uppermost on a pad of folded newspaper; cover one half of the leaf with the yellow felt pen, working from the centre vein outwards and following the leaf shape as before. Directly this has been done, scrape the edge of a ruler over the damp surface thus removing excess shine. Complete the other half of the leaf in the same way. The reason for doing one half at a time is because the felt pen dries very quickly and the area must be scraped with the edge of a ruler while still damp. Leaving the leaf on the pad of newspaper, mark the veins on the topside using a wooden cocktail stick, or the pointed end of a knitting needle will do. *See Fig 13.16* for vein marking. Cut small scallops out all

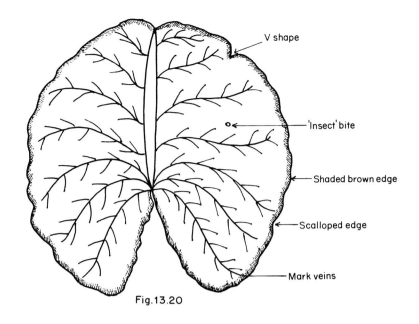

V shape

'Insect' bite

Shaded brown edge

Scalloped edge

Mark veins

Fig.13.20

round the outer edge of the leaf, plus an occasional 'v' shape. *See Fig 13.20*. Using the brown felt pen, colour the outside edge to a depth of about $\frac{1}{16}$ in. Do not make this a hard, straight line round the edge, but a slightly broken, natural brown edge to a leaf. Likewise, apply brown felt pen to one half at a time (topside of leaf only) and scrape with the edge of the ruler as before to remove excess shine.

An occasional 'insect' bite may also be added: make a small hole with the scissor points, and twirl the brown felt pen round the edge of the hole. The remaining two leaves are prepared in the same way.

Take three paper strips 4 in deep × $1\frac{1}{2}$ in wide (which were cut out with the leaves) and paint one side only of each piece using sap green, and applying the paint as thickly as for the topside of the leaf. Put on one side to dry thoroughly.

Cut three lengths of fine plastic-covered wire ($1\frac{1}{4}$ mm thick) each 6 in long. Prepare each one as follows: cover the whole wire with a narrow strip ($\frac{1}{4}$ in wide) of leaf-green crepe, winding it round and sealing with spots of glue. Measure $2\frac{1}{4}$ in from the top of each wire and mark with a felt tip. Cut strips of paper tissue $\frac{1}{2}$ in wide, and wind them round the stem, commencing from the mark, and pad the bottom half of the wire until it measures $\frac{3}{4}$ in circumference. Use frequent spots of glue when padding and also check the measurement is accurate, e.g. do not make the stem too thick. Cover the prepared paper strip with glue on the unpainted side. Lay the padded stem onto this and roll it firmly round, overlapping the edge. Press between fingers until the glue has set. When quite dry, rub the yellow felt pen over the painted surface. With the seam of the padded area of the stem on the underside, paint glue along the top portion of the stem and affix it to the unpainted centre vein on the back of the leaf. Fill in any gaps either side of the vein with a little sap green paint if necessary. Turn the leaf over and rub the centre vein with fingertips to make it stand out. Bend the stem of the leaf as shown in *Fig 13.21*. Prepare the two remaining leaves in the same way.

Bend the stem of the lily to form a large hook, twist the end of each of the leaves round the hook and squeeze them together using the pliers. Bind them all together with strips of the floral tape. You may find it easier to bind two leaves only then add the third as it is difficult to hold three in place at once! The leaves should be evenly arranged round the lily and as they are bent they support the flower.

Hook leaves round
flower hook, squeeze together
and bind with floral tape

Fig. 13.21

14. Ivy Trail

Materials

White typing paper, A4 size (71 g/m^2 quality)
Rose wires
Leaf-green crepe paper
Thick yellow felt-tip pen, ($\frac{1}{4}$ in wide)
Sap-green acrylic paint No 348 (Winsor & Newton)
Paint brush with fairly stiff bristles, ($\frac{1}{4}$ in hogshair)
Dark-brown pastel crayon
12-inch ruler
Lead pencil (B)
Sharp scissors
Thin card for templates
Tracing paper
Adhesive (Latex-type)
Jam jar lid for mixing paint

Variegated ivy
Leaf-green pastel crayon
Colourless nail varnish

Fig 14.1 Ivy Leaf patterns

Cut card templates of the ivy leaves from the patterns given in *Fig 14.1*.

Lay the templates on a sheet of the white paper, and draw round each leaf with a pencil. Cut the leaves out of the white paper. Cover seven rose wires with a $\frac{1}{4}$ in wide strip of leaf-green crepe paper, secure with spots of glue as you wind.

    Commencing with leaf A, glue one end of a covered wire down the centre back of the leaf. Likewise, glue a wire down the centre back of the remaining six leaves.

Assembling the ivy trail

Take leaf A and leaf B, paint a small amount of glue along the side of the A stem about 1 in down from the base of the leaf, leaving about ½ in of stem at the base of leaf B, and affix alongside on the glued area. *See Fig 14.2.* Cut the stem off leaf A, and use the remaining stem B to extend the trail. Bind the joined area using the leaf-green crepe strip.

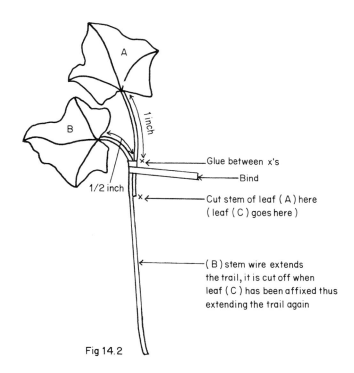

Glue between x's

Bind

Cut stem of leaf (A) here
(leaf (C) goes here)

(B) stem wire extends the trail, it is cut off when leaf (C) has been affixed thus extending the trail again

Fig 14.2

The remaining leaves are joined on in the same way, on alternate sides graduating in size from A to G. The length of the trail may be increased by cutting more leaves of each size, e.g. three As, three Bs and so on.

Each new leaf added extends the trail, and the stem of the previous one is cut off as shown in *Fig 14.2.*

When the trail is completed, proceed to paint it as follows: squeeze a small amount of sap-green acrylic paint onto the jam pot lid. Apply a fairly thin wash of paint to the back of each leaf, do not use much water as the paper becomes soggy and crumpled. When the paint on the back of the trail of leaves is dry, apply a much thicker amount on the topside. It is better to mix the paint on the lid with a little water, apply one coat and then another on top when the first is dry. Make sure the brush strokes are from the centre vein towards the outer edge.

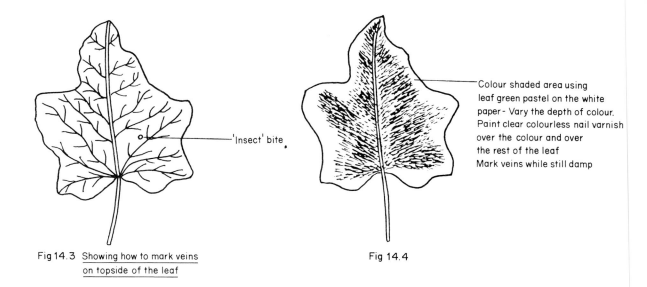

Fig 14.3 Showing how to mark veins
on topside of the leaf

'Insect' bite

Fig 14.4

Colour shaded area using
leaf green pastel on the white
paper - Vary the depth of colour.
Paint clear colourless nail varnish
over the colour and over
the rest of the leaf
Mark veins while still damp

When the painted leaves are quite dry, using the thick yellow felt-tip pen, colour on top of the paint as follows. Do only one leaf at a time as the felt tip dries very quickly. Brush the felt tip over the painted surface of the first leaf, working from the centre vein to the outer edge, as previously described. While the leaf is still damp, lay it on a pad of newspaper and using either the point of the scissors or a wooden cocktail stick, mark the veins as shown in *Fig 14.3* on the topside of the leaf.

The yellow felt-tip gives the leaf a shine, and if marked quickly the veins stand out well. 'Insect' holes and blemishes may be added by making a small hole through the leaf and brushing the edge of same with the dark brown pastel crayon.

Each leaf is thus completed and the ivy trail arranged in a natural twisting trail.

VARIEGATED IVY

Assemble an ivy trail, and colour the white paper as shown in *Fig 14.4* using a leaf-green pastel crayon. When the leaf has been coloured, a coat of colourless nail varnish is painted on top. The veins are marked while the varnish is wet so do one leaf at a time. The result is very realistic and long lasting. The backs of the leaves are not coloured, as the colour would show through and spoil the effect. Ivy trails are most useful to cover up the mechanics of floral displays.

15. Ideas for Display and Storage

Fig.15.1 <u>Straight and stiff, sparse foliage</u>

Fig 15.2 '<u>Growing from central point,
plenty of leaves</u>

The following ideas for display and storage of the paper flowers in this book have developed during the years I have been teaching and exhibiting. Flowers made from paper which are often mistaken for real have to be displayed with care to maintain this illusion. A convincingly realistic rhododendron may have a few fallen blooms at the base. On numerous occasions I have overheard two visitors arguing about a rhododendron display, one saying to the other 'But they are real, look at the fallen blooms!'

To make a fallen bloom, make a bell-shaped flower only, glue round the bottom inside edge and gather it in loosely. No stem or stamens are necessary.

Likewise, a rose with a few petals scattered beneath it will really make your friends think it is real! The petals should be No 5 size, and bowled and curled to the rose-petal shape.

Spring flowers such as daffodils, narcissi, crocuses, primulas, may be displayed in bowls or flower pots filled with real bulb fibre. To do this, first dry the bulb fibre. Spread a suitable amount out on a tray or tin lid and place in a warm dry place for a few days.

PREPARING THE POT

Place a few pebbles in the bottom to weight it down, wedge a section of oasis on top, then add a piece of chicken wire over the oasis. Finally fill the container with the dry bulb fibre. The crocuses, etc. may then be 'planted' by pushing the stems into the prepared bowl or flowerpot.

A common mistake when displaying daffodils and other similar flowers is to arrange them singly and too symmetrically so they look unnatural. *See Figs 15.1 & 15.2* for the wrong and right way. Another mistake in similar displays is to have too few leaves. Leaves may be time consuming to make, but they are as important as the flowers. It is the leaves which act as a very important backcloth for the flowers.

The Water Lily   The water lily is a very attractive centre piece for the dinner table. Place it on a circular mirror, and it reflects beautifully. A mirror tile may also be used in this way.

Flowers displayed out of season   A bowl of daffodils on display in the summer months is not a pretty sight! All flowers especially paper ones should be packed away when they are out of season.

IDEAS FOR STORAGE

Good cardboard boxes may be obtained from the supermarket; empty shoe boxes are ideal for storing smaller flowers. To prevent crushing the flowers, thin cardboard collars may be made and fitted under the flower head. *See Fig 15.3*.

The cardboard tube inside a toilet roll is perfect for the anemone; thread the flower down through the tube from the top. The tube protects the flower and enables you to pack a good number in one box. The crocus also fits well into the cardboard tube.

Naturally, all paper flowers must be stored in a dry cupboard as any damp will spoil them. In addition strong light will fade the crepe, so always place your display in a corner of the room away from direct light. If these tips are observed the flowers will last for months and be a constant source of pleasure. (Some of the flowers displayed in this book are several years old!)

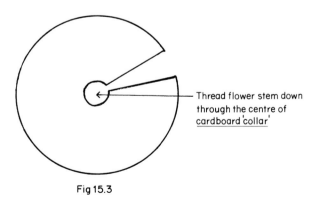

Thread flower stem down through the centre of cardboard 'collar'

Fig 15.3

Index